Gods
Posts

Truth Lives in us All!

RUSSELL HARPER II

Gods Posts
Copyright © 2023 by Russell Harper II

ISBN: 978-1639457373 (sc)
ISBN: 978-1639457380 (e)

All rights reserved. No part of this publication may be reproduced, distributed, or transmitted in any form or by any means, including photocopying, recording, or other electronic or mechanical methods, without the prior written permission of the publisher, except in the case brief quotations embodied in critical reviews and other noncommercial uses permitted by copyright law.

The views expressed in this book are solely those of the author and do not necessarily reflect the views of the publisher, and the publisher hereby disclaims any responsibility for them.

Writers' Branding
(877) 608-6550
www.writersbranding.com
media@writersbranding.com

Table of Contents

Acknowledgments v
Biography of Russell James Harper II vii
About the Cover viii
Preface ix
The Eye of a Storm 1
Close to Home 4
The Battle from Within 6
The devils job description 9
The Interpreter or Intercessor 11
Lost but Not Forgotten 12
Coincidence? Not in My Vocabulary! 20
The Lord Is with Us 23
The Unseen 29
Always Proof 32
To Those who Feel Lost, but Are Not 33
The Holy Spirit Is Like 36
Corrective lenses 38
The Importance of Friends 40
Our Bestest Friend 41
The stranger at the table 44
These truths are indeed self-evident 46
Sugar, Spice and Puppy Dog Tails 48
Jesus Loves the Little Children 50

"It Could be Worse" 52
Pointing Fingers Anyone 54
RAW 57
The "Ordinary," "Out of the Ordinary" 62
Fishin Without a Net 64
Sunrise-vs-Sonset, Did You Ever Wonder 67
GIFTS 68
Now That's What I'm Talkin' About 72
Are You in Doubt? 74
Ya Ever Get the Feeling You're Bein' "Watched"! 76
What Is This World Coming Too 80
What God is that Perfect Word 84

Acknowledgments

This book is dedicated to the Children of God and the gifts that they are using for the expanding the body of Christ through our Holy Spirit. My Mother and Father who took me to church and introduced me to God Jesus and the Holy Spirit through the Bible. To my Lovely and faithful wife of 44 yrs., the mother of our three children and numerous grandchildren. I thank our heavenly father that through fervent prayer, conviction and the ultimate truth he has led me to the writing of this book inspired by his whispers and inspiration throughout my life.

Also, the Bicycle shop sisters, Mother Lovely, and her three daughters Victorious, Princess and Precious, that showed me that there can be revival anywhere in Christ and that wearing the right shirt can open endless conversations of our Lord and Savior!

To my Prayer Pastor Paul Covert, a true friend, mentor and Author as well he wrote "Threshold" and "52 ways to pray."

Another author whose books I could not put down is Mark Batterson who wrote the Circle Maker books.

A young lady by the name of Victoria Porter Cramer who fought and beat cancer and wrote the book "Living Life Loudly".

Numerous singers on K love radio such as Laura Daggle, Ray Stevens, Toby Mack. There are probably hundreds more, but it's like the making of a good Marinate sauce; You could use thousands of ingredients and never remember what they are, but the "meat of the matter, is Its all Good!"

Biography of Russell James Harper II

I grew up in the country of Ohio and was raised in a Christian atmosphere and attended Church and went to Church Camp for 3 or 4 years. It was there that God made sense to me, that was where I got a young but meaningful AhHa moment. I could not get enough of the Bible and sermons. I joined the Navy before I graduated in 74 and enlisted a month after. When I did my 4 active I knew it was time to settle down with my childhood sweetheart but during a layoff I returned to the Naval Reserves and retired from steaming boilers after 24 years as well as from my current civilian job at Mansfield Plumbing Products at 22 yrs. We moved from Ohio to Arizona where my parents are and I worked with a Defense Company, Nammo Talley INC. for 20 and I am now happily retired as is my wife. I am a Prayer Warrior at Central Christian Church of Mesa, we have 3 grown Children of which two served in the Navy Wesslee, Desiree, and one Crystal who has been a wonderful Foster family for children in Ohio.

About the Cover

I wanted to depict, that all of us have forgotten, or ignored our journey of Faith in some way or for some reason.

"We are posting our sins to the cross," the cross that was, and is, only a symbol, of remembrance of how, and why Jesus Christ died for our sins.

What Jesus did that day, but most importantly is doing for us even now, seems to be buried in the sands of time, almost forgotten.

But it's in the right position to be picked up and carried as the scripture says in Luke 9:23, "Whoever wants to be my disciple must deny themselves and take up their cross daily and follow me."

Preface

There is a page in this book that you will own up to! Your issues are nothing new, God has and does see it all and you are not alone!

We are all sinners and fall short of the Glory of God. Romans 3:23

Even though you already have accepted Jesus as your Savior and we strive to be like Jesus through our salvation, we still sin, we are living in a fallen world

[20]But our citizenship is in heaven. And we eagerly await a Savior from there, the Lord Jesus Christ, [21]who, by the power that enables him to bring everything under his control, will transform our lowly bodies so that they will be like his glorious body. Philippians 3:20-21

Therefore if anyone is in Christ, he is a new creature; the old things passed away; behold, new things have come. 2 Cor. 5:17

[16]For God so loved the world that he gave his one and only Son, that whoever believes in him shall not perish but have eternal life. [17]For God did not send his Son into the world to condemn the world, but to save the world through him. John 3:16-17

Are you lost? Do you think you're not good enough for God? That you can never, ever get there from here because of what or who you have become? Or even though you have accepted Christ into your heart at some point in your past and you've gone way out of bounds with Jesus, you are thinking He probably doesn't want you back! You think that your sin is soooo down and dirty, that there is just no way that anyone, much less, Jesus, could ever love you or me.

Do you use the word Backslide to describe the problems of your life, or when a friend wants you to pray with and for you or when he or she asks you to go to church with them?

How long will you ignore those tugs that tell you "He wants you back and he still loves you"? Does that word Baggage mean more than packing for a trip, and the words excess baggage means you think you are over Gods weight limit for departure?

YFICA

Your **F**riend **I**n **C**hrist **A**lways

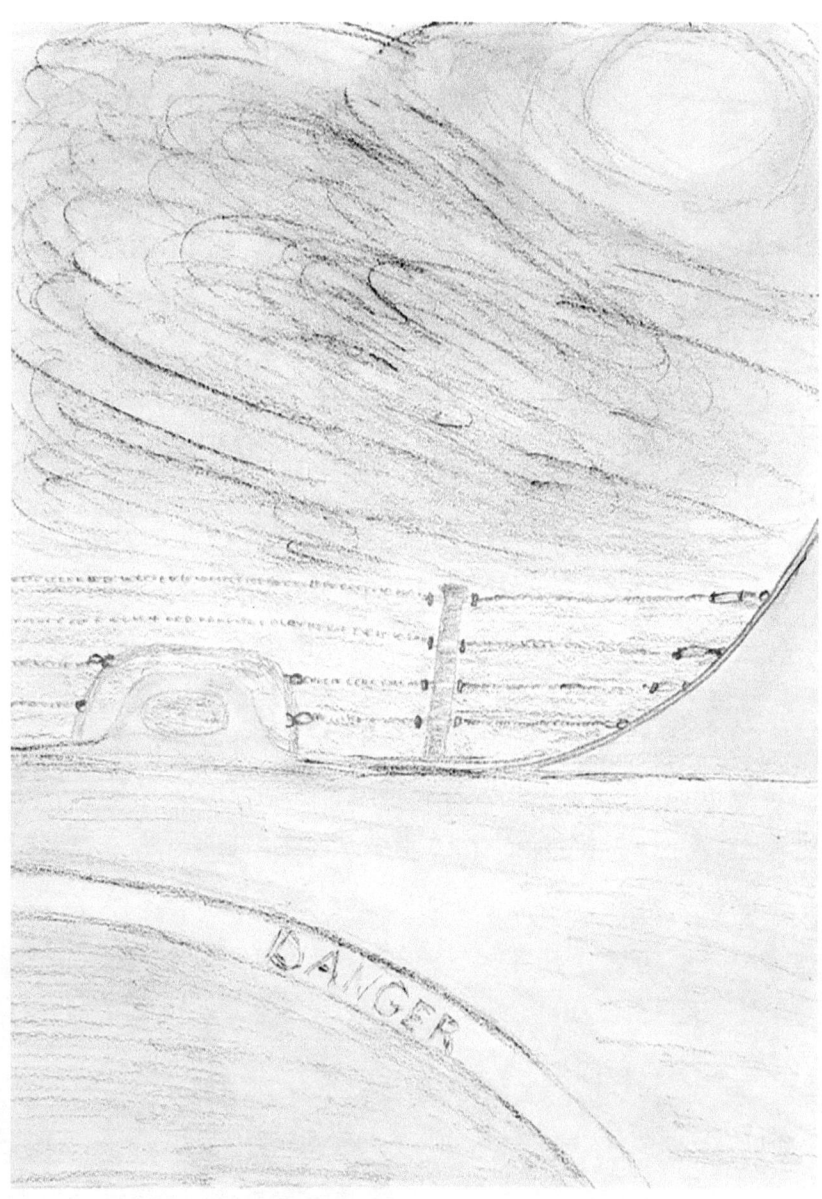

The Eye of a Storm

I heard the song "Eye of the Storm" by Ryan Stevenson, the other day.

I started thinking about my Navy days. Back in 1975 I saw the eye of a storm in the middle of the night, we were going through a Typhoon! I was young, [19] as a matter of fact and thought, at that time, that this Destroyer, (my home for about four years), was indeed my sanctuary and was invincible. The USS England was 533 feet long, 54 feet wide built of iron and steel through and through and weighed 7800 tons. I was one of the few that worked in the most dangerous place in the ship, the Fireroom! Picture a sealed coffee pot full of water and steam and now its rocking back and forth.

There were ten to fifteen of us for each of those two spaces. Our ship was rocking back and forth to the tune of about 25 to 38 degree rolls.

Well let's get back to the storm. Our mess decks were being tore up in preparation for a yard period so when I had to get from one fireroom to the other I had to go topside I held on pretty tight to those lifelines and that's when I saw the eye of the storm it was like we were out of it but then I looked up at the sky and it seemed like I was looking through a big tube with the moon in the middle. It was sorta still out and the temperature was tropic. I knew I had to get back to the other fireroom so I went on down. About that time the rocking got vicious again and like I said, I was young back then and this was just another adventure to me. It turned out that I indeed had seen the eye of the storm, It was rough getting into, calm in the middle and rough getting out of that storm off the coast of Korea, all those years ago.

One thing you learn going into a storm is it's a rough decision to go in, but sometimes you can't go around it. Then we are given an eye or time out in the middle of it, on our way through It prepares you to go through to the other side. "One thing I forgot to mention about these storms, Typhoons, Tornadoes, or Hurricanes, is that these storms travel and if your moving in the same direction you will find yourself in that storm a lot longer, unless it dies out."

The storms of life work the same way; going into them are rough, painful and sometimes hurtful. If you get to the eye you have the time to reflect on things that have happened, how you got there, how you get out, and time to heal before moving ahead. Then you have to exit, "push through to the other side," you learn from the situation and choose the right direction to leave it so you're not in there any longer than you have to be and end up at the right place so you don't end up on the rocks or run a ground, or just end up sunk.

Whatever you are going through, whatever pain, sin, loss or turmoil is crippling you, we have someone on the inside, through the rough times or through the eye of the storm and He helps you through the rough times coming out of any and all situations that is in your storm.

Before you start saying to yourself "this is my storm", "I own it," "it's my grief, "or "you don't know what I'm feeling," Think about this; The one who gave it all, yes I said ALL, and may I remind you of that story. About the Storm of all storms, the real "Perfect Storm," Gods only son Jesus went through that storm and planned his entrance and exit before any of us were ever born. It wasn't an easy escape, but one that will never be forgotten all in the name of Love.

So do you think your storm is so bad, that you can't give it to the one that can take your burdens completely away, do you think you've done something so wrong that Jesus Christ sacrificed himself for a pick and choose?

[1]John1:5-10 says [5]This is the message which we have heard from Him and declare to you, that God is light and in Him is no darkness at all. [6]If we say that we have fellowship with Him, and walk in darkness, we lie and do not practice the truth. [7]But if we walk in the light as He is in the light, we have fellowship with one another, and the blood of Jesus Christ His Son cleanses us from all sin. [8]If we say that we have no sin, we deceive ourselves, and the truth is not in us. [9]If we confess our sins, He is faithful and just to forgive us our sins and to cleanse us from all unrighteousness. [10]If we say that we have not sinned, we make Him a liar, and His word is not in us.

All of us need to know, Jesus loves us in our bad times and our good, no matter what the hurt, loss or sin is or was.

I have seen the eye of the storm and my storms, I gave it all to him and that's the end of it, that's all the reminders and baggage that come to haunt us. We just give it all to him and let it go.

YFICA

Close to Home

Have you ever read a message or heard a message and it "accurately" described exactly what you were going through at that very moment?

It's like buying a car and all of the sudden you start noticing all of the same cars on the road "just like yours."

In the Lords way, those messages are not just meant for you! They are, through the Holy Spirit, meaning something to everyone but because the Holy Spirit in you is interpreting it for you, it will not be the same for everyone else. I guess you could say it's a custom fit, sometimes it gives you praises and sometimes conviction.

It's the Lords learning curve, that's just the way it works. It just happens to Hit you close to Home and for what Jesus the Christ did on the cross for us, it should!

The Battle from Within

Have you ever found yourself in a constant battle, in your mind with temptation? It's that inner self that says, "As long as I keep this to myself it doesn't matter." That's when the conversation between good and evil begins. Friends, we have all been there, whether its food, drugs, sex, or the craving of a TV show, it doesn't matter; they are all called idols in the eyes of the Lord whether seen or unseen, yea that's right just like the golden calf in the Old Testament, in the eyes of our Lord, they're all idols.

It's that one more piece of cake or I'm going to do it this one time, oh and here's the biggest lie you tell yourself, are you ready? Brace yourself because you're going to think I was there when you said it. The famous, "I can stop this anytime I want to" or "I can turn it off like a switch"! Yea sure you can. The devil is on top of that game, he can be quite tricky. He knows all your weaknesses; he knows all the things that go on in your head, things that waste your time when God has other plans for you. The things that side track your plans just long enough for you to forget or lose interest.

Through all this, God knows it is going to happen because he gave us something called freewill. That was given to us because of the first sin in the garden of Eden. He wants us to come to Him of our own free will. He wants us to ask and depend and trust in Him alone and to deal with the all this temptation, all the idols, all of this *self*.

1 Corinthians. 10:13 New International Version (NIV):

> [13]No temptation[a] has overtaken you except what is common to mankind. And God is faithful; he will not let you be tempted[b] beyond what you can bear. But when you are tempted,[c] he will also provide a way out so that you can endure it.

Now here's a good question: if we all have that voice in our heads and you would have to be lying if you said you don't, for those of you that claim to be, or are atheists, out there. Why would you not believe there is a God speaking to you as well that would be unseen or unheard to any other person but yourself? You may call it your conscience; I call it the Holy Spirit! Whatever you think it is or isn't, it is telling you what is right and what is wrong! To me that is God's guidance and that is the Holy Spirit.

Read these scriptures, these are written for all of us these are undeniable truths.

2 Corinthians. 12:7–10 (NIV):

> [7]or because of these surpassingly great revelations. Therefore, in order to keep me from becoming conceited, I was given a thorn in my flesh, a messenger of Satan, to torment me. [8]Three times I pleaded with the Lord to take it away from me. [9]But he said to me, "My grace is sufficient for you, for my power is made perfect in weakness." Therefore I will boast all the more gladly about my weaknesses, so that Christ's power may rest on me. [10]That is why, for Christ's sake, I delight in weaknesses, in insults, in hardships, in persecutions, in difficulties. For when I am weak, then I am strong.

Ephesians. 6:10-18 (NIV):
The Armor of God

> [10]Finally, be strong in the Lord and in his mighty power. [11]Put on the full armor of God, so that you can take your stand against the devil's schemes. [12]For our struggle is not against flesh and blood, but against the rulers, against the authorities, against the powers of this dark world and against the spiritual forces of evil in the heavenly realms. [13]Therefore put on the full armor of God, so that when the day of evil comes, you may be able to stand your ground, and after you have done everything, to stand. [14]Stand firm then, with the belt of truth buckled around your waist, with the breastplate of righteousness in place, [15]and with your feet fitted with the readiness that comes from the gospel of peace. [16]In addition to all this, take up the shield of faith, with which you can extinguish all the flaming arrows of the evil one. [17]Take the helmet of salvation and the sword of the Spirit, which is the word of God.
>
> [18]And pray in the Spirit on all occasions with all kinds of prayers and requests. With this in mind, be alert and always keep on praying for all the Lord's people.

Also:

Philippians. 4:8 (NIV):

> [8]Finally, brothers and sisters, whatever is true, whatever is noble, whatever is right, whatever is pure, whatever is lovely, whatever is admirable—if anything is excellent or praiseworthy—think about such things.

The devils job description

We all know the word that describes what can keep us out of Heaven and away from the one who created us, only three letters that spell sin, right? So if we could subtract one thing from our lives, from this world, that would prevent all sin in our lives, what would it be, desire, want, or would it be temptation?

I would say temptation that would eliminate the very thing that brought sin into this world. Would removing the very thing that caused sin eliminate sin? Well if there were a job description for the devil that one word Temptation would be the word to describe it.

"If" and I say "If" we could rid this world of sin it would be a better world and we would be closer to heaven. I'm not saying it could happen, we cannot do it, alone, we need the love of a father, one that put his only son on this earth over 2000 years ago. Jesus sacrificed himself for our sins, He came to this world to show us that just like he can take away affliction from man and woman, such as the gift of sight to the blind, take disease away in the blink of an eye, make the crippled walk, he can and has taken our sins away for all time past, present and future with the admission that we believe that he died on a cross because he loved us that much. When we ask his forgiveness for our sins, He will separate those sins from us as far from the East is from the west. (Psalm 103:12, "as far as the east is from the west, so far has he removed our transgressions from us."

Doesn't that make us love our God even more? He wants us to put everything into his hands and love him with all of our hearts, souls and minds forever, that is the greatest commandment.

No we could never do away with sin, for we have all sinned and fall short. But knowing the key ingredients we can ask God to help us stop sinning.

The devil came into the garden as a snake and introduced us to temptation and it has plagued us ever since. Let's fight against it by recognizing and turning it over to Jesus Christ and let him put the devil in his place.

YFICA

The Interpreter or Intercessor

I realized something the other day while doing our
Bible Study in the morning.

When people ask us to pray for them, or with them, the Holy Spirit
is moving between the two or more of you.
He is speaking to all of those in attendance.
So he gives all of you the words for that prayer in order
for it to reach God's heart.
If you say okay and walk away, you are depriving the message of the
Holy Spirit. Thus you, or we are depriving God the
opportunity, the glory of answering that prayer!

So that brings the scripture of Matthew 18:20 full circle when it
says, "For where two or three are gathered in my name,
there I am among them."

Lost but Not Forgotten

Have you ever been lost? No, I mean really lost. Not like driving down the wrong road and not knowing which way to go. I found a new meaning to "all roads lead to somewhere!"

When I was young, back in Ohio where I was born, I grew up in the country. I found paths in the woods, dirt roads, and creeks that lead to nowhere. I would get lost and find my way back one way or another and there was water everywhere, farm to farm; woods to woods. Heck I'd make my own paths if I couldn't find one.

I was brought up to be prepared for any, and everything about survival thanks to my grandparents that went through the Depression.

Ya know people talk a lot about the Depression, but more of us need to learn about that kind of survival! My Gram-ma would make up these little cans with matches an rolled up newspapers, maybe a tootsie roll, in case I got lost I'd have something to get me back, a fire to keep me warm or a light to guide me.

Now my dad taught me similar things that were more on the fix it side of things. He went through the Korean War with the navy on a destroyer. He taught me how to shoot, fish, and care for a rifle, and a pistol. He showed me how to fix a car, truck, or anything else that had wheels or tires, electric, water, or anything mechanical.

The one thing I learned from my mother was that there is a good Lord that loves us. I think I came into his arms when I was about thirteen and like Samuel I realized he must be talking to me in a church camp on Vespers Hill. It all made sense after I quit playing in the dirt listening to all those messages day after day, year after year in that Church Camp Otyokwah in Butler, Ohio. Finally the day came I woke up in front of a makeshift cross from a couple of small tree limbs in the center of a concrete slab raised up from the ground about three or four foot high and it was shaped like a cross on the ground.

A lot has happened since then; I lost my way here and there but never lost sight of Jesus and never denied him, but just went by the wayside.

I joined the navy and got a little more lost—well that was about to take a whole new turn. The word "lost" just gained a whole new meaning for me...

I'm not so young anymore, I'm a bit forgetful, and I don't live in Ohio, I live in Arizona. The hills are mountains here and water isn't that easy to come by. There are a lot of animals I like in Arizona, but the rules change a little when it comes to being careful. Things I wouldn't give a second thought of back then, "well let's just say, they give me a little eternal scare today."

It happened on March 21 a couple of years ago, myself and a friend of mine went out to scout for turkey to prepare for the season to hunt them. It was up north of Payson at a place called, of all things, Turkey Point. We were scouting for trees that they roost in so we would have a starting point to follow them the next morning. We found a tree on a north ridge and we sat up there and called to them with box calls and everything we had in our bag of tricks for about two hours but no luck. So we went back to the truck and went back to camp, had a good dinner using a small grill with mesquite charcoal, really good we almost over ate.

Our plans were simple for the next day, get out to the spot we were at today before the sun came up and listen for the turkeys to fly down from the roost of the tree. This usually happens at sunrise, which is later than normal because of the Mogollon Rim.

After a good night's sleep we got up with plenty of time we decided to change the plan to cover the possibility that they were on the other side of the road. So my buddy went on the north side on a peak and I went to the south side peak where we had decided to start originally. We waited for the sun to rise then we listened for them to fly down. Nothing on my side looked down where we parked could see the truck so I knew I was where we were the other day. I started calling for the turkey to answer . . . nothing. Our plan was to check it out then meet back at the truck and call from there to locate them as to what direction to go. Heck it was my plan, "I was the experienced turkey hunter!"

The plan started out good, until I decided to venture out to the other side of that point, you know, "the point where I could see the truck." That's where the confusion started. I think I forgot to mention the plan was supposed to be simple. So according to the "plan" I didn't think to charge my phone when we hit the sack, I also drank all of my water before I walked up the hill, mountain, whatever you called it, and I left my pistol in the truck. "I did have my camera." I have no idea why that seems to be important to this story except it just goes to show us what we sometimes think is important. My thoughts were an hour, maybe two, to scout and then go back down to the truck and get back to camp.

Well I went back up a slope trying to get my bearings and things just didn't look right, I didn't see my markers. I had seen a pink ribbon tied off at the very top, "not here," I remember a bench shaped log I had been sitting on right on the peak, nope not here. I walked off in another direction thinking the tree I started out at would be just up ahead, instead I ended up at a literal drop off that looked to be about two hundred feet down.

I finally decided to sit down to rest, I could feel dehydration starting to affect me, I was getting cotton mouth, and my throat was getting dry.

I was on the verge of panic, and then I started to hear a whisper, you might think "voices in my head," "disillusionment," no it hadn't been long enough for that! It had only been about an hour but that would be about three hours without water, so I did what I had been taught out of the manual "the Bible." I got on my knees and prayed out loud, clasped my hands together, and raised my arms up in the air and loudly said, "Lord, Father in Heaven, keep me calm, give me wisdom in this time of need Lord, I am praying and asking in the name of Jesus please get me through this." Afterward I quickly started thinking of survival techniques I had read about, saw on programs, or just came naturally; you know last resort stuff. Of course the first scripture that went through my head was:

> *Ps. 23:4 (ESV): Even though I walk through the valley of the shadow of death, I will fear no evil, for you are with me; your rod and your staff, they comfort me.*

The story of Jesus and his forty days in the desert, made me realize that fear is evil, just as it would have been when the devil tempted Him. Granted this was no desert, and this was no forty days, good grief it wasn't even noon yet, but still no water for even this amount of time was no picnic. Climbing up and walking down mountain sides for any length of time will dry you out quickly as I found out.

I was really open to listening for the Holy Spirit's guidance and through it all he was telling me "this is another journey of survival and trust." "Survival was telling me the unthinkable would be necessary." If I was lucky I would hold out another hour before I passed out from dehydration.

At one point I ran into a four-wheeler trail, either direction I went lead me nowhere. I came to another drop off and stood there looking at a clear shot of the Mogollon Rim, it was beautiful, you would think with that really nice camera I would have taken a picture wouldn't you, didn't even cross my mind. I guess I was just too focused on the end game, and listening for instruction from above.

It had been a while, so again I spoke to our heavenly Father. "Dear Heavenly Father, I can't keep this up." I said, "Please show me where I can find water."

I might add I had this song from a certain Christian radio station in the back of my head the whole time, it wouldn't go away, it was like the whistling of the theme to a certain TV show. I was still calm, I was still on a mission! I had checked what I had on me before, but now was a good time to check again. Let's see, a wooden box call for turkey, an expensive camera, totally useless for survival, "maybe pictures of water would help," naaa, a coat with a hood, a homemade wing bone turkey call, slate call with the striker, wallet, three knives, two pocket and a hunting knife on my belt. "So far nothing to make water!" Finally I look over one of the peaks and I see a bare spot in the bottom of the crevice, where the two hills meet, another possibility that the Lord had given me. Getting down there would prove to be even more work, "It was a little steep."

It was steep but not as much as others I'd already walked down, there were a lot of fallen trees crisscrossing each other all the way down. I started down the hill sorta thinking of my knees. I walked like a skier sidestepping all the way down to the ravine keeping my attention on my left knee (that's the artificial one), and I'd been taken care of the other one so I don't mess it up.

When I got there it looked hopeless at first but then I heard him say, "It's there, you are gonna have to dig to get to it." So after a good look around for snakes and spiders and such, I scooped out under a small drop off in the creek. It started to get damper and wetter with the more I dug. I had dug out a hole about the size of my fist and there it was seeping out of the hole a little at a time. Yes it was muddy and it smelled like a sewer. I cleared it as best as I could but now I needed a cup or something to drink out of mouth to water wasn't working. So I reached into my pocket and I felt that slate call, boy I hate messin' up a good turkey call but "hey" you do whatya gotta do. I busted the slate out of the dish, it still had a couple of holes in it, but that was the best I could do, then I cut half of my hood apart and used it like a strainer. I soaked the rag really good and filled the little bowl up and started following the crevice to find where it leads to. Sure enough I ran into a fence that leads to a cattle creek full of creek water, cleaner water. I felt like I had been in death valley all day and drank and drank 'til I had, had enough.

I decided to follow the fence around to find out where it lead to, and as I walked keeping the fence in sight, I noticed that in the opposite direction there was a mansion of a house with a few buildings. But it looked to be about two, or three, miles off. I made a mental note of it and decided to follow these marked trees that I thought would take me to a ranger station or at least to a nearby road. As I walked in the opposite direction for about a mile following a fence, I thought I heard a couple of four wheelers on the other side of the fence so I crossed and began yelling for help; they either never heard me or they didn't care so then decided to cross back and head back toward the house I had seen, it was quite a ways off but I figured I didn't have any other choice. I was growing weaker and weaker from the lack of nutrition.

So I followed the fence back to the creek and started drinking the water again. It felt a little better but hunger was the problem so I did what we all do in a tough situation, normally it would be a last resort, but God never left me, he was there the whole time. So I asked him Lord what do I do for food, I think it's an issue now. Once again he put scripture in my mind:

Matthew. 6:31–33 (NIV)

> *³¹So do not worry, saying, 'What shall we eat?' or 'What shall we drink?' or 'What shall we wear?' ³²For the pagans run after all these things, and your heavenly Father knows that you need them. ³³But seek first his kingdom and his righteousness, and all these things will be given to you as well.*

I started looking for edible things and my country thoughts from Ohio kicked in "grass," if I had too, but I started to see something I hadn't seen for a while, except in Ohio, "of course I hadn't been this desperate before either," there on the ground smaller than I'm used too, were dandelions, at least a few full handfuls.

These would last me, "maybe," until I get to that house. I pulled them up and got a handful at a time and started to chew them up. I could feel the energy building up. But it was still a long walk. Water was not a problem if I got thirsty again because I was right by the creek that leads to the lower part of the house where they had made a pond. There was a gate at the edge of the pond and I was really hesitant to open it and go in, but again I didn't care at this point so I went in and I followed the grass around the pond to the hill up to the house. I heard two little girls playing on their tricycles in the large parking lot by the vehicles. I stayed away from the entrance of the house. I was coming outta nowhere so I didn't want to appear to be a threat to them. I asked the girls to get their dads or their mommy. I think I remember them asking me if they could help me too, but I would prefer that they get their daddy, so they did. By then their mother came out and looked down from the wrap around porch at me and asked if I was okay. Her husband came out and they asked me what happened. I proceeded to tell them and they asked me if I would like something to eat, and seeing an apple on the table in the kitchen, I asked for that and then they let me borrow the house phone. I tried to call everyone but as my luck would have it, or as the Lord would have it, another page to the story had to run the course, I could reach no one. They asked me where we had camped; and after I explained in the best detail I could, they stopped me and told me they just went through there that morning and described everything that we had set up including Freddie's truck. They told me that I had traveled quite a distance to get there. After that I gave the rest of the family my thanks and both the husband and his brother put me in a four-seated, four-wheeler and took me around a definitely shorter way then I had taken to get to their house. When we finally got back to the camp, Freddy was not there so they went up the road a little, about where this all started and there was Freddy on his phone; dare I say he was just getting ready to call the rangers when we showed up. I learned many things that day, I learned to appreciate things that God has made and the way he made them, I learned to appreciate the way his plan worked for me and for others I come in contact with. I learned that God is an unseen voice that exists everywhere but most of all he is always, in us, and he is constantly walking right beside us!

Coincidence? Not in My Vocabulary!

Have you ever said to someone or thought "that was just a coincidence"? Well this is not just a story, it's not just a coincidence! I do not believe anything is a coincidence, especially when it concerns life, death, or the hereafter. By the way there is no hereafter, I think people are confused as to what that actually means. It should be rephrased the "after here"!

When I was at work just a few months ago, I had to kill a little time before reporting back from my last round for the day (I am a security guard now and had been a little too perceptive in too little a time); not only that, but the freeway was blocked and we had to go the long way around to get from one place to another. I decided to go to Walmart and visit my wife real quick and see what time she got off work. It was on the way and it was where we picked up our lunch earlier. My visit was brief, but I had the company truck and I didn't want to stick around too long. On the way back to the truck, I saw all these pamphlets on the ground like someone was in a hurry to leave and dropped them in a hurry. I thought for a moment that they were just advertisements, but upon a closer look, I realized they were Christian tracts that never made it to the windshields of the masses in the Wally World parking lot.

On the front of the tracts read "What's Next After Death" and a picture of a graveyard. I almost threw it back down or walked it back to a nearby trash can but a friend of mine, I should say "a brother Christian of mine" that just recently moved away gave me some advice in a roundabout way, "these words stuck." He said he picks up any tract he sees, "Ya just never know who it'll be meant for." So I picked up one of the tracts and stuffed it in my pocket and headed back to the guard shack.

This is part two of the story!

When I get back to the guard shack, we sat around waiting to get relieved for the day. My partner was bored, he's somewhere in the vicinity of seventy to seventy-five. Well what I thought was going to be a conversation to save for the night hours to put me to sleep, shook me, and made my very soul take notice as he brought out a conversation that I was not expecting. It started out about old coworkers we knew that had long since left, or died, or retired. I knew the one that he brought up, and I knew the story behind his hospital visit that took him away from work for quite a while. So when he started talking about him, my ears perked up like a dog bein' called to supper.

This particular coworker had a number of injuries that caught up with him after all the years of working with a back injury and had to do with a fusion of the spine! I remember it well because he told me in very specific words what had happen. When he was rushed to the hospital the last time for an emergency operation, he died on the table and had an out-of-body experience and he described it to the point that he wasn't afraid to die; he said he really wasn't sure he wanted to come back. That's right I knew the story he told me about the out-of-body experience and that's when the Holy Spirit took over the conversation. My friend's ears perked up when I told him the story that he didn't know. This is something that all of you should pay attention to if you ever run into the situation and care for that person as we should care for all those that are lost or trying to find their way back. He said he is really interested in this stuff but he doesn't go crazy about it. He said I just want to know where or who I will be when I die; heaven or hell, will I come back as a monkey or somebody else. He didn't know what to believe in, he was referring to the Hindus and reincarnation, or whether he would go to a heaven or a hell.

I started to tell him there is no reincarnation when you die. Die, die, that word resonated in me. I said, or rather the Holy Spirit said to him, "You know this happens to me every once in a while." And then I handed him the tract I picked it up in the parking lot. He started to read it. I told him, "Apparently it belongs to you. It's dealing with exactly what you are talking about. It's yours. Keep it."

He told me he was a good guy. He's not a bad guy and that's when I told him good or bad, "works" won't get you to heaven. I told him I'm not gonna shove it down your throat. We have all sinned and fall short of the glory of God, and we will continue to sin. Do you know we sin every day just by speeding in our vehicles every day?

This is a true story. Do you believe this is a coincidence? I don't know about you, but I know Jesus Christ lives in me and His words and actions are guided to and through us by the gift of the Holy Spirit, that he gave us when we accepted him as our Lord, and Savior. I know that because He died on the cross for my sins and for anyone's sins that accepts the truth and believes in that truth and asks him to forgive his sins. A song that a lot of us grew up with tells us about this truth, His truth. The chorus goes like this:

> Because He Lives
> I can face tomorrow
> Because He Lives
> All fear is gone
> Because I know
> He holds the future
> And Life is worth the living
> Just because he Lives

I am praying for this man, my friend, and I'm asking you "Do You See Coincidences" or future brothers and sisters in Christ that just don't know they're way hungry for the truth that are hungry for the Holy Spirit, the very words of God?

The Lord Is with Us

After reading about halfway through Mark Batterson's book, *Circle Maker*, my personal prayer circle started with an interview for one of two lead jobs. It was October of 2013. I had applied for this job before, but for another plant, this time it was for the areas I worked in most of the time.

I decided to circle the plant three building with prayer every day until the interview. I remember walking into the room calm as a cucumber, that day I asked the Lord to choose my words wisely, be honest and sincere, no matter what question came up. I wasn't going to reach for answers. I mainly wanted this job to rid myself of the stress and pressure of striving to reach a level of perfection that turned out to be a battle between management and the ever changing measurements of quality. "Nothing was good enough anymore," and I had workers under me that wouldn't listen because I didn't have authority over them as a lead would.

I went in with a positive outlook and I left feeling free because I knew God was there with me in that room. Well I didn't get the job, but that was all right as I was pleased with who did get it.

Well about a month went by and the job I was on was not quite finished but my stress was all but gone. I was working a little slower because I was the only one left on the job. They had to move the others to a more strenuous one where they needed more hands. I gave them 110 percent on every stage of the job I was working. I didn't know it then but things were about to get really bad.

I trusted the Lord and prayed through everything every day; I know the Lord had given me a break. He saw the stress, knowing that I just couldn't give up; he also saw me and Cathy reaching out to help some of the others cope with unemployment.

I believe that God saw the potential to my loss of work and more time for Him, so much so that I was let go with about thirty other coworkers. Now, I know what it feels like to get that kind of news at the worst time, but through the time I was off, he filled me with a calmness that felt so right. He wanted me to spend quality time with him, learn more, and listen more. It was like my taste buds for him were new and everything I felt from this point on was a new experience. I walked out of that room with a smile on my face. The only regret I had was for the others and those left behind that would be handling the load with less people. I also hoped that they realized what the company as a whole was going through, with the economy, the downsizing was just good business. This was a bad time for a lot of us, I always told everyone I worked with, "Never pay any attention to rumors and don't spread them around, it's just not healthy." It's seed for the devil, oh don't get me wrong, I've fallen into that trap before! It's really sort of a surprise when it finally happens to you.

For some reason, God was telling me that day to be prepared for a change, that's right, he told me "I'm changing your life once again." I kept trying to figure out what this was all about, "Yea like I'm going to figure God out." I remember thinking it had something to do with our tithing because we just recently decided to give at least our 10 percent and do it without questioning our finances at all, or maybe it went further back.

I remember Cath and I had a heart to heart about convictions that I had. They needed to be told to her, no matter when, no matter what, or how bad or trivial it was. "Everything," even before we were married thirty-six years ago, it had to be told. I knew in my heart that we are one in the flesh and I would not be free of any sin until that was done. The Holy Spirit was heavy on both of us that day. It was hard to spill my guts like that; to tell the Lord alone and asking forgiveness was one thing, but that higher power was telling me, "How can you be whole if only part of you is forgiven and the other part didn't know why?" Now I know what Jesus was doing when he would repeatedly say, "I tell you the truth." It is all he could do because Jesus Christ is Truth.

Whatever it was, it was God's plan, so my life was changing again. Well, I walked out with the others, we gathered our things from my locker and then took the "long" walk out; as I got to the line of people, some I worked with for a long time, some just a few years, some leaders and planners, and some just like me, the Holy Spirit said to reach out to them, they were hurting too. With tears in my eyes and some of theirs as well, I hugged each one of them as I went down the line and told them it wasn't their fault, I don't blame the company either, we'll make it all right.

I got on my motorcycle and headed back home. As I pulled into the driveway, I saw Cath and Paco, our dog, step outside. Cath said, "What are you doing home so early?" I said with a smile, "They finally let me go, and you know what, they couldn't have picked (I stopped myself), no, 'God' couldn't have picked a better time for it to happen." I told her how the Holy Spirit talked to me this morning on the way in, so I was sort of prepared when it happened. I was really happy because I felt God did speak to me, so I told Cath we need to get in touch with two of my coworkers; the Lord say to me, "These two need us more than ever." So I called them, said we need to meet right now and how about we go to the Dirt Water Springs restaurant. Let's have dinner and talk things over, we'll buy. So we met there and after prayer, we all talked out what was on our minds. We eventually got the blame game over and moved on to the "where do we go from here" mode. They both said that if we hadn't called, they were getting ready to pick up a bottle and drink it away.

One thing I decided to do was write an email to all those I worked with including management as well. I told them again that I understood what needed to happen and I would continue to keep them and the others that got laid off in my prayers. Then I expressed my gratitude and appreciation for the time that I worked for them.

The company was good to us, at least I always felt they were good to me, after leaving a job of twenty-two years in Ohio to be with my side of our families out here. This place treated us pretty good and when we left, we got a good fair package.

They met with us in a lobby and set up classes for us to create or update our resume. We were even served dinner between the day's activities while we were there as well. Our insurance benefits paperwork was set up for unemployment. They also got us to sign up for courses to enhance our careers for a better chance to get a job.

I made good on the time I had off. I learned a lot about the state programs and what had changed from fifteen years ago, that was "the last time I made out a resume." Most of us stayed connected through the Workforce Connection while Cath and I continued helping some of the others the best we could. One friend of mine from an earlier lay off was still having a hard time getting a job. We prayed a lot for him and his wife for a job and finances.

His story with me was one day at work he was having trouble with a couple of coworkers and he was stressed out. It had happened a couple of times and it was having an effect on his health, as a matter of fact his heart. One night I got the feeling the good Lord wanted me to talk to him, so on my break I caught him alone at work and asked him how he was doing, he just let it all out. I prayed for him and I did something another friend had done for me, I reached into my pocket and gave him a coin that had a prayer on it. I told him to carry it with him, and any time he felt down, pull it out and read the prayer on it. I told him not to blame anyone for anything, just ask the Lord to handle it and walk away from it. He still carries it as far as I know. Sometimes a little nudge, even from an inanimate object like that coin can help someone remember to take it to God.

It wasn't long after that he was let go and shortly after that he experienced a mitral valve problem. I, as well, just happen to have that same issue that he had. I had just learned how to deal with it since I had discovered what it was and if I'm not careful I might end up with the same surgery.

I got the calling from the Holy Spirit to follow through with him and we should not stop comforting him, especially now, and be there for his wife as well. We went to see him in the hospital prayed with them, gave him confidence that the Lord is going to be with him through this and that he has a plan. During one visit after work, I saw him lying in the bed and he was having a hard time sleeping. He was sort of squirming around in the bed and told me he was having some issues with the medications. I reached out, held his hand, and he gave his life to the Lord that day. I seriously think after we talked about some things in his life, he was handling things better and was getting a little sleepy. He had a few issues after that but the surgery went well. Later they had to go in and replace the valve and he is doing a lot better. He even ended up with a job not long after he had recovered. We continue to keep them in prayer.

Then there were "the four," Mom and three daughters, who were the proud owners of a bicycle shop on Main Street in Mesa. After my knee replacement surgery, I needed to get some real exercise going after about six months, so we decided to get a bicycle. When we walked in, the first thing they noticed was the shirt my daughter in Ohio had bought me. It had Jesus on the front "Yellow on Black," it was a real conversation piece. I rather enjoyed that as it opened up more conversation about our faith and our Jesus. It sent a message to anyone who saw it. Well God intended us to cross paths because we couldn't stop talking about our faith and Jesus, as it turned out to be the ultimate Christian bicycle shop! All this because I wore my Jesus T-shirt to church one day and believe me I never wear a T-shirt to church. We walked in and it was like we knew each other all our lives. We just inspired each other over and over about the Lord and his plans for all of us. It wasn't long before I was stopping over helping them fix up their bicycle shop, doing this or that and talking about our Savior. It was one of the hobbies I had for quite a while.

It would get to the point where I would get about half of what needed to be done because we would always end up bringing out the Bible; reading and teaching each other about God, but we turned out some good work and did it with the help of our Lord as well. We grew and learned in both fields, and teaching them how to do a lot of woodwork on their own. Like I said, there were four of them, the mother and three wonderful daughters. I would see her husband and he would help out every once in a while when he wasn't hurting from arthritis. He is a lot like me, a "Prayer Warrior." The Holy Spirit was filling the areas of our life during the time we were together. It was always a revival while we were together, but as good things go they had to slow down and eventually I couldn't get over there anymore as God still had a plan for me. You see, the same company that let me go decided to call me, so I put my resume in which turned into an interview for a security job at the same place.

I was getting too comfortable at the bicycle shop and yes, God had other plans. It turned out to be less work, a lot less stress, no more painting and no more straining to please people that had no direction to go with the product.

God had put me in a position to talk to more of my fellow workers and grow in the word and faith with other Christians as well. My insurance was replaced by the Veterans Administration since I had a disability from the time I spent in the navy. I was considering it for the next year so there was no cost issue. I lost no time because it had only been three months and my pay was sufficient. I hardly complained about my pay anyways. I was happy not just because I got a job but because the evidence of God and my faith was constantly being proven. The Holy Spirit was and is running ramped in my life and I am sooo grateful to him for saving me from the muck of this world and making me an alien to it. I am a follower of Jesus, the Christ, and not of this world. Praise God the Almighty, the Great I *Am*.

The Unseen

Roman's 1:20 20. For since the creation of the world God's invisible qualities—his eternal power and divine nature—have been clearly seen, being understood from what has been made, so that people are without excuse.

I am confused over the thought that there are people out there that don't believe in God because he is not visible or because they do not see his works being done! I have mentioned the word "Analogy" in before in my writing.

The definition of: Analogy: a comparison between two things, typically for the purpose of explanation or clarification.

When I read the Lutheran Hour Ministries lesson today the Lord spoke again to me about this. "Yes the unseen Lord," the Holy Spirit. I have mentioned the obvious before: If you are educated in anything there is an analogy for it somewhere. My simplest example of an analogy comes from being an engineering minded person, something simple, for instance, If you bought brand new batteries for a flashlight, and you change them out for new ones, you would expect that flashlight to work, you would assume or trust that that flashlight will work; Why? How can you be sure? You have developed a "Faith" in those batteries and that flashlight.

Hebrews 11:1 Now faith is confidence in what we hope for and assurance about what we do not see.

When you plug in an appliance that you use every day, you're sure it will work , your positive.

You drive your car every day, you could've driven it a minute ago and you seriously believe it will start and run and take you wherever you want to go. That is faith without even blinking an eye!

You see the clouds, you feel the humidity, you see rain coming down 5 miles out, coming right toward you, "let me stop here for a second." I live in Arizona you can be right where I'm describing and never get rain in this situation; for some reason, God just must think It's got to go somewhere else. It will stop within feet of where you are and you could step in and out of it or it will blow right around you. Anywhere else it would be pouring. Kidding aside, anything is possible with God, anything, even rain in Arizona.

Hebrews 11:6 And without faith it is impossible to please God, because anyone who comes to him must believe that he exists and that he rewards those who earnestly seek him.

Now some people believe in Heaven and Hell, some think there can be one and not the other! First off they're can't be one without the other!

When you were a kid did you ever get rewarded for something? Ice cream, stay up late or let's not forget you can play your video games, (news to me, but then I have grandkids), now if you did something wrong and got caught there's the infamous "go to your room."

The analogy? "Heaven or Hell" vs "Good or Bad." The only thing different here, is with Heaven you not only believe in Heaven and Hell, you got to believe and accept Jesus Christ and what he has done to keep you out of hell. Jesus Christ who is God in the flesh came here for that reason and he loves all of us. After all the sacrifices throughout the old testament to compensate for sins, his was this one sacrifice to draw all the sin from whoever believes in him and throws the freewill that was given to us out and choose to be with him after the end of our earthly life.

Prov.3:5,6 5.Trust in the Lord with all your heart and lean not on your own understanding; 6. in all your ways submit to him, and he will make your paths straight.

He deserves our lives for what he did for us. God may be unseen, but just as we have a spirit which is also unseen and heard from as well, he created himself as Jesus "God in the Flesh" through his Spirit and that Spirit has a name The Holy Spirit which he freely gives us when we decide for Jesus the Christ. He then gave that life knowing he would be raised from the dead.

There are so many things in this world we put our trust in, things we see and things we don't, how can anyone deny God and believe in tangible's. Do you remember what love felt like at first? Try to remember that and then multiply it by everyone in the world and then think about how Jesus feels when someone walks away from him. The bigger the body of Christ the more love he has for us.

YFICA

Always Proof

There have been those times that
I don't hold back if I get a prompting to talk to
someone about whatever the Lord wants me to or write.
When I get that feeling I
know I can't stop writing until He is done speaking to me
and no one can convince me
that this is not the Holy Spirit working in me.
The exciting part about these experiences,
is, it is so overwhelming to me that his power and love
for me is proving time and time
again that he is right there with me all the time.
My heart has been hardened because of the sins
that I have been convicted of after all
this time. Now after confessing and leading a life for Him
this proves to me that his
saving grace has never let me go.
I help those who feel lost because they feel
that they're not worthy even if they are born
again He shows me how to help them find their way back the
same way he has shown me.
We are never forgotten, and this is the proof
that we all need to hear! We all sin and
fall short of the glory of *God*. Thank you, Jesus,
for the sacrifice you have given for us
and thank you for the gift of the Holy Spirit!

To Those who Feel Lost, but Are Not

While reading our Prayer Pastor Paul Covert's book, *Threshold*, I was reminded of some friends of mine that I met through our conversations about the similarities of our convictions from the Holy Spirit.

The Lord always seems to lead me back to this scripture when I think things are too hard to handle or when I'm battling with memories that I just need to give to Him. So I read again 2 Cor. 12:7–10. It's about that thorn in the flesh.

When a friend has something in common with you; for instance, you were both in the military or you both have kids in the same school, etc., etc. You end up sharing stories of whatever it is you have in common. You also find out through your conversation that you were both at one time or another "Born Again Christians," you both received Jesus Christ as your Lord and Savior at one point in time, or one of you is not a Christian and guilt starts coming out of the conversation.

While emptying your hearts out to each other, memories come out about things you did in the past. Some are what you or they would think is "really bad" and some are what you might have thought not that bad at all. One thing throughout this friendship you should keep in mind is to trust each other and always keep that confidence between yourselves and the Lord. Even if you are not a Christian and keep in touch, don't make that person out to be worse than yourself, "all" have sinned and fall short of the glory of God. Not just the ones you talk to, it means you too, we are not to condemn anyone!

You want them to be comfortable in talking to you so you can help them, just as it will help you keep in step with the Lord. You may not remember from your newbie Christian past, but this is when the Holy Spirit is at his best. Jesus Christ is right there with you waiting to reach out and help you through this so you will receive his loving kindness. He has always been there with you but now you can see, now you can hear and now you will be more aware of him. This is when you should and will hear that still small voice!

The sins that you have kept bottled up are coming out because you are sharing your feelings. It is good to share, God loves you and he doesn't want you punishing yourself any more than you do. He is trying to speak to you through the Holy Spirit and through others.

Now... you have a battle going on between the spirit and the flesh. You have come to that point where even things in your childhood may be convicting you. It may be something small or a sin that you may think is unforgivable, you have tucked it away thinking that it would just disappear, but now your sharing it and your conscience, which is the Holy Spirit from Jesus is convicting you to give it all to him, ask forgiveness and walk away from it. Again this is where the battle begins, this is where you either fight back the devil and the flesh, tell the Lord "I need you," and then you confess, ask forgiveness, and live it and don't turn back.

Or you can continue suffering with the dread of living with this sin that you have bottled up inside you for even longer. The devil is winning! Not just because you decided to walk away, but because those around you, family and close friends may never know the truth and the love of Jesus Christ and you may be allowing them to suffer as well.

They might think that it's okay to live a life of sin! They might decide not to accept Jesus as their Lord and Savior and their soul will be lost. We are the light of the living God, we don't hide it and we do not live out a life of sin. He has a plan for us all.

We are all sinners and fall short of the glory of God, but as Christians, even though you may have lost your way, you must remember our saving grace is that Jesus Christ died for all your sins for all time. He has always been there to pick you up and show you the way, all you need to do is talk to him, ask him. You need to pick up that Bible and feed your soul again. Do you remember what that felt like, it can be that way again it can be that way now. It says in the Bible there is only one unforgivable sin, just one, and that is to deny Christ as your Savior or the Holy Spirit which is the very breath of God himself.

The bottom line is this:

The fact that you feel guilty, shameful, or just bad about something, anything that you've done or said proves that he has not given up on you, he doesn't forget about anyone. He is waiting for you to come to him. He is there with open arms waiting for you to come back, because he loves you unconditionally.

    When you are broken, the Body of Christ is broken.

The Holy Spirit Is Like

The Holy Spirit is like a small bird that whispers in your ear and sometimes he's like a roaring Lion. He pushes you like the small child that wants you to go somewhere with them or he is like the raging river that throws you to the nearest coastline. He knows what you want to hear but never speaks it. He knows what you need to listen to and that is the voice of God you will hear.

What you want, VS what you need, There is a phrase in a song that is so uplifting in me. It is about the line that is where the sinner and the saint meet, when that line is crossed it slides behind, and moves further to the back of the sinner, and it's washed away like the tide pushing further in to pull you closer to the Father's love.

Sometimes when we listen we see a wealth in knowledge as to what his plan is. Sometimes we are directed, to "redirect" to a place we would never want to go, but the gift of listening is just that, a gift, and it strengthens us in the fact that God always hears, and always answers. He is alive in me, in you. I use the word inspiration like water running out of a spilled cup, because it doesn't stay in me. The Lord has streamed words through us as a vessel that never empties.

When we choose not to listen to him because of doubt, the story goes even longer and that is okay too, because there is a purpose no matter how big or how small. Sometimes its long journey because eventually it will touch more people's lives. Sometimes it's just a short one, to get the attention of a few. It comes in the form of conviction and it comes in all sizes, some will cut to the bone after years of hiding, or it can come out immediately after your eyes are open to it. Listening is the key, facing it, and asking forgiveness is the answer.

How does someone get your attention do they whisper? Are you listening, or ignoring? *Do* they yell, because you don't see that train wreck coming at you? Do you keep walking across the tracks because your mind is made up?

The Holy Spirit is the breath of God, and Jesus delivered it to us, in person. What were the instructions on the box? Turn it over what did it say, "Are we letting those tiny whims sit in idol or are we still waiting for the fuel to light those fiery tongues that were so powerful in the day that they were brand new?" People when we accept Jesus into our hearts the Holy Spirit is brand new in us. Sinning is the last thing that is supposed to be on our minds. Everything in our garage, in our minds, our buildings, our driveways, and in the store windows is no longer supposed to be a necessity.

We go back to that one word that launches a thousand ships or a word that can cause a disaster for thousands of people. With God we can save people, without we can slip into a coma to the rest of the world! Free will is given to us from the Lord to show us that we will make the right choice into to God's will.

Corrective lenses

I was inspired by Chuck Swindol's message this morning it stood out when he spoke of David and his nemesis Goliath of Gath. Nothing inspires me more like the story of David and Goliath. It's like the story of Captain America; this scrawny guy attempt's Joins the Army and is the most unfit guy you could imagine.

A lot of us can relate to him. Some of us have been there, and something just doesn't fit in the mix. Those so called misfits have something none of us are prepared for, they have a blind dedication, they don't know it right away but others will see that person the one that is told to stay down, give it up or go home, they stand up to the most impossible barriers, they all but lost battles like David. Now what was Davids transformation, 1 Samuel 17: 41 Meanwhile, the Philistine, with his shield bearer in front of him, kept coming closer to David. ⁴²He looked David over and saw that he was little more than a boy, glowing with health and handsome, and he despised him. ⁴³He said to David, "Am I a dog, that you come at me with sticks?" And the Philistine cursed David by his gods. ⁴⁴"Come here," he said, "and I'll give your flesh to the birds and the wild animals!" ⁴⁵David said to the Philistine, "You come against me with sword and spear and javelin, but I come against you in the name of the LORD Almighty, the God of the armies of Israel, whom you have defied. ⁴⁶This day the LORD will deliver you into my hands, and I'll strike you down and cut off your head. This very day I will give the carcasses of the Philistine army to the birds and the wild animals, and the whole world will know that there is a God in Israel. And you know the rest.

A young orphan, Steve is attacked by bullies in Hell's Kitchen. However, Steve's resiliency, despite his small stature, inspires a young James Barnes to come to his aid and fight off the bullies. The two then become friends. Now Captain America was used in an experiment that turned his physic into a hero's welcome, but we see our destiny in a much smaller way, we look past the strong guy, the bully that blocks the door or the devil that tempts our every thought and blindsides all of us at one time or another.

When I go into a junk yard most people see wrecked and twisted metal cars and trucks. I can't help but see things that can be fixed and better than they were. Sounds a little familiar doesn't it glasses correct our line of sight and Jesus is looking for all of his people and his specialty is those that are scrawny, broken, suffering and yes sinners like us all.

YFICA

The Importance of Friends

This week went pretty well one of my brothers in Christ at work was dealing with guilt really bad. Our talks really inspire me because it's like we are connected in some way.
I'm either prepared before he comes to talk to me or we are both struggling with the same sort of issue.
The situation this time was sort of a reoccurring one, sin that he has already asked forgiveness for, haunts him once in a while and this was one of those times. I think we all go through this at one time or another; I know I do and I dismiss it to the Lord after I make a thorough prayer search of the matter. Speaking to others with the help of the Holy Spirit inspires me more and it is invigorating to my faith in Jesus Christ. It's just like we have all the tools and wood for a project, but we just don't know what it is yet. We should know that God knows what it is we just have to take the long way around to figure it out. He took the instructions out of the box because he is making us write them as we go!
I was told by the Holy Spirit this time to tell him that the key is listening and acting on what the Lord's plans are for him. When he is sure that he needs to act, then and only then will he be comforted. I'm certain the devil will slip in and out, but the Lord's timing will always be in place.

Our Bestest Friend

Love has different paths, love of a mother, love of a father, brother, sister, love of God! There is a love that reaches deep into your bones, that is so sacred, that lips cannot speak. Only in the book that God gave us does that love come out so elegant. A story that starts with armor, sword, and bravery. It's a story that I think explains why man is mentioned so often back then in the Bible.

I woke up from a dead sleep with a wife that is flesh of my flesh in my bed and I felt a closeness to a friend like a love that I have never felt anywhere but with the deepest of friends. I am afraid at times to explain but God has reached me this morning to put to paper this friendship, this kinship, that love has reached to love a friend in ways that God loves us. I want none of the ugliness that this world has made of it, for it is not the love of a man and wife.

This love started in the garden of Eden; I feel, between God and his first human creation, Adam, he is so proud of his creation, that a love was formed, a closeness to a companion, that everything in word and deed could be shared understood, and agreed upon.

Then came Abraham, Joseph, Moses, Noah, and all the prophets, that God loved and they did love him so intently that every step they took was for His purpose, and no other not even for themselves prophets like Elijah, Elisha, Jeremiah, and all those that are written about throughout the Bible.

One particular story stands out that bears the fruit of my thoughts, is the story of David and Jonathan they were so close of friends that they shared their thoughts, and dreams, their hunting and fighting instruments, and instruments of music, but most of all David shared his love of the Father God with him.

God competes with the life he gave us; and when David grew older and he falls into sin God never forgets that love as David reaches out as he did in his childhood thus bringing the true statement that would be spoken by Jesus some 1500 years later as he spoke to the ones he loved dearly the only way to enter the gates of heaven is as a little child.

So was the love of God and man, so was the love of Jesus and his disciples, so was the love of God and David, and David and his love for Jonathan; but most importantly in his youth and his older age returning to God's love and once again love and friendship have reached the same line. For God so loved this world, for God so loved man, "his creation," for God loves all his creations but not as he loves the human race that he made in his own image.

I woke from a dead sleep thinking of all this, and the one gift that God gave us after his departure from this world, "the Holy Spirit." He spoke to me once again, He brought a friend to mind that drew me to his words as he does so many times

I thought of a particular friend that I was far from for a long time that touched my heart as he did in an earlier part of my life. There are so few a friend that are so close, and life has a way of walking them away from us. How I hurt thinking of what God has felt when we have walked away from him. The sorrow he goes through when his best friends that he loves with so much compassion move away, or drift away for a time or to never be heard from again.

Have you ever loved someone so much that you have stepped across that line to take his or her place to do what needs to be done, have you ever seen the outcome of people that understand right away what is going on at that instance. The story, the life of that story, your story is being passed on to those around that figured it out. The love of the closest of friends, it's there don't miss it, it will come back just as it was when you were young. Jesus loved his disciples, and he told them to love us as he loves us, because he is God and God is love and he knows where we come from, and he knows where we are going, he's just waiting to see how we handle it, and how we let him handle our destiny and that is where are heart truly is.

For God so loved the world that he gave his only begotten Son, that whosoever believes in him will have everlasting life, not life on earth, not love of a man and a woman, the life that man was introduced to when he saw Adam, when he saw David. When David saw his friend Jonathan then the love of those dedicated prophets that loved him so much. For in flesh God wanted to feel our love, and give all that love and in that flesh died for us all of us, just as our death will be so that we can be with him, with God where it all started.

What would you do for your closest friend in the whole world? What makes you hurt when your friend is gone? What makes you ache when your friend is in pain? Multiply that by millions trillions and ask yourself; what did Jesus feel like looking down at us from that cross that he loved this much so that he could be with us for eternity. What did he feel on that cross, betrayal, denial, rejection, loneliness? Always remember He was God on earth. He made the connection for us, and he had to go through all of this. He knew the outcome. For he loves all of us and we are to love Him with all our heart, all our soul, and all our mind and we are to love everyone the way that we want to be loved, and to even love our enemies. So who is your Jonathan? Who is your David? Who is your bestest friend?

The stranger at the table

I saw a table, a large oval table and people of the earth seated there.

There were those from nations all over the world.

I saw all religions the soldiers, the sailors, people that were hated and some that were loved.

There were Presidents, Kings and Queens, the rich and the poor; the homeless, the lost. There were Mothers and fathers, brothers and sisters, battered wives and husbands some bad some good.

Those that wanted forgiveness and those in disbelief. There were even some that claimed that nature had wronged them in their existence and those that believe themselves to be something they're not. All these around the table and at one end they're, "as on the road to Emmaus", sat an unrecognizable, stranger with his hands stretched out in front of him dressed in clothes of ancient times, sandals on his feet and a kind look upon his face and yet he appeared to be blind.

When the pointing of fingers stopped and the clambering of words went silent, the man stood and his words went out before them but his voice was heard from another that was unseen within the room.

He said in a soft unoffending voice "my sight of you I cannot see here on this land or this world, I only see the soul of all and not in this realm but that of the home I have provided for thee. The Love for all you see is of the heart and soul when you give it to me. You are all created by me, my Father and I. There was never meant to be color, race or creed. You are all Brothers and sisters to me unless you decide to deny me, my Father and I.

YFICA

At this some fell to their knees and others fully prostrate themselves to the floor weeping because their eyes had been opened. Some would still have nothing to do with him, while others could not understand because there eyes and ears still would not allow them to see, to hear, that this was truly the Lamb of God his only son for this visit was the three in one.

CNM

These truths are indeed self-evident

The sermon we listened to on Sunday was so good that this is what I felt I needed to share on Martin Luther King and this the day we recognize him.

The good Lord put some on this earth as a reminder of the ongoing works of God and his Son Jesus Christ or God on Earth. Today also shows that Truth, Love and Peace are forever in need and at the last calling it will prevail.

The fight is not over, there is no rest for the wicked and we must always be on the ready. For we know that in our Bibles it reads" Jesus is the Way, the Truth and the Life," that is found in John 14:6. It also says in John 8:12 that "Jesus is the light of the world." It seems to be more magnified in these days of darkness, those days have always been around us, and yet there are those still lost that choose to stare and not ignore or turn toward that ever present light that has always been offered, we only need to come alongside them and introduce them to our Lord and Savior.

What ever happened to those people, where have they gone where have we gone? "We are the Hands and Feet of Jesus the Christ because he is not here in the flesh but always in the spirit; This spoken by yet another that is no longer with us, Mother Theresa. He wants us all eventually with Him.

Those that have bore the burden, as in the song that reminds us "Abe, Martin and John" were only what seemed temporary to us as they all strived for a total love and freedom through their words and deeds. Their direction was misread and misunderstood; Kind of sounds like someone that we know that suffered the ultimate sacrifice for something no one else could erase but Jesus Christ himself!

So what have we learned from them? The same as we have learned from God our creator. There is no color, no race, no hatred in those that truly believe in our Lord and Savior! We are one in the Body, one in the church, we are the bride of Christ and we are" Not of This world!"

YFICA

Sugar, Spice and Puppy Dog Tails

My wife Cathy always tells me about the people that grace her place of business; she has that spark that attracts people, to ask her for prayer, that want to talk to her because of her kind words, and the little kids that come into her vision center and say things like this little 3 or 4 year old girl, she just blurted out to her that she likes glasses and swimming but now it's too cold.

When is the last time you remember that kind of innocents? We all need reminders like this, If you ever get a chance, make time and make it a point to talk to a 3 or 4 year old. Rarely do they tell you things they don't like. They will however tell you things at random that they do like; puppy's, swimming, playing with frogs or playin dress up and makeup and cowboys and Indians

What do us adults usually talk about hmmm? We seem to talk about things we don't like more often then we think. It seems to be the norm and that's too bad.

I remember a Tom T. Hall song called "I love" He said things like, "I love little baby ducks, Old pick up trucks, Slow movin trains and rain". I could just imagine him talking to a child or a grandchild with these words.

In Matthew 18: 2. He called a little child to him, and placed the child among them. 3And he said: "Truly I tell you, unless you change and become like little children, you will never enter the kingdom of heaven.

Therefore, whoever takes the lowly position of this child is the greatest in the kingdom of heaven.

A lesson, if you want your children to grow up and be nice, caring and loving people keep this scripture sharp in your heart and mind the Lord will keep it in their souls.

Little boys are made of Snips and Snails and puppy dog tails, Little girls are made of Sugar and spice and everything nice.

YFICA

Jesus Loves the Little Children

When I grew up I didn't see many black people, In my neighborhoods, no "actually now that I think about it, I don't know whether I did or not." It's probably like that because we as kids don't see a difference, unless a hateful, or dislike happen within the parents and rests on that child concerning race. There it is that word when I grew up the word race had to do with cars, running, the Olympics etc., etc., etc. When did that change? Did it have something to do with the *human race*? So where is that finish line? What is the purpose of the finish line? And are we sure we are running in the right direction? I would have to say from my perspective and throughout my life it is indeed taking off in its own direction.

While I will have to agree to the facts, that we moved into this country by choice, one way or another. The black people were forced into this country one way or another as history has it. I don't know how it came about exactly, but at one time the lands were all connected so we are, as I firmly believe descendants of the same families that were on the ark. So between that and the Tower of Babel we have differences in a lot of things as the cultures and places of living moved on. Doesn't knowing that make us more aware? More caring for one another? I guess not except those of us that are truly religious minded.

Well back to me and the way I was brought up, I never did understand the difference except the obvious way of speaking, "some more than others," color of the skin, "some darker than others," and I never treated anyone any different than myself because there not. I grew up in a school where

I had a really nice friend, a girl named Bonita. I really liked her. When I went into the navy, I worked right beside a lot of black friends that worked just as hard and we all went to town together, ate together, the same things that "our race" do when we went through hard times—we cried together, we laughed together, we backed each other up in all ways, we put our arms around our friends no matter what color they are.

My dream, not Martin Luther King's dream, but my dream, is to go to all the places we are having "Racial Tension," (got to be politically correct these days), like Ferguson, and ask anyone black or white or whatever their race may be one question and know, that they heard that question.

I would like to ask each and every black or white or any and all "races" that are having tension in this world, but for now just here, where we are so hateful and mad at each other. Do you know a little song called "Jesus Loves the Little Children" and then remember and sing the next line loud or in your heads doesn't matter; but if you get it, the Lord God almighty just might say what we should all know by now, God has not forsaken us, He has not forgotten us, and He does love all the little children of the world. Jesus loves the little children, all the children of the world. red and yellow, black and white, all are precious in His sight, Jesus loves the little children of the world.

"It Could be Worse"

These are hollow words for someone going through a rough patch. They fall prey to someone who wants to give a short excuse with quick advice. You want to escape the reality of it all or want to side step a long explanation or conversation for a see ya later I gotta run attitude. This should never be the case especially for the Christian/ Follower of Christ. It could be that you have a situation that you just don't feel like owning up to on the same issue, If that's the case maybe its time that the Lord has sent someone to knock on your door and you should stop, listen and think this one out before dismissing it. Maybe its just a timing issue? Either way they don't know what you are thinking because you are in such a hurry that you don't take the time to sort it all out.

It is meant well, but the thought of the hurting an individual, is that you need to move on to something else that is more important then they're problem.

My first thought in all this is; how many times have I done this exact same thing? We never want to pass judgment on ourselves or others, it's not our job, and the next thing is; How would we feel if this was reversed? Think about the worst place you have ever been, have you ever had a moment where you needed a comforting word, a caring hand, or a whisper of encouragement?

What did Jesus say about this?

Philippians 2:4 do not merely look out for your own personal interests, but also for the interests of others.

Romans 12:10 Be devoted to one another in brotherly love; give preference to one another in honor;

John 13:34-35 "A new commandment I give to you, that you love one another, even as I have loved you, that you also love one another. "By this all men will know that you are My disciples, if you have love for one another."

1 Thessalonians 5:11

Therefore encourage one another and build up one another, just as you also are doing

This is not something that I am writing for any particular situation. The Lord put it on my heart to share and for me to learn by. While the implications are somewhat something to think about; that indeed, "things could be worse," We need to treat all people with the fact that we should act and care for all people as Jesus would. So I ask the question of all questions "What Would Jesus Do WWJD," this is not just a bumper sticker or another good line, we need to live it!

Just as "Things Could be Worse" is a truism, it is not what Jesus would call compassion by a long shot. YFICA Russ WWJD

Pointing Fingers Anyone

Are you ever offended by people that point you out, that say you or him or her or she? Yes it is very offensive to point at others and say they, him, her, or she did it; or it was they're fault.

Mark 2:16–17:

> [16]When the scribes of the Pharisees saw that He was eating with the sinners and tax collectors, they said to His disciples, "Why is He eating and drinking with tax collectors and sinners?" [17]And hearing this, Jesus said to them, "It is not those who are healthy who need a physician, but those who are sick; I did not come to call the righteous, but sinners."

When it comes to sin, "we" have all fallen short of our walk with Jesus, all of us and that cannot be reversed, we need to accept it, ask the Lord for forgiveness and turn away from it. Like a child burning his fingers on a hot stove they learn not to do it again... but this is much more than burning your fingers this is how you live your life this is what will become of you we will all have lessons/ problems, shame, death, life, birth, tragedy, persecution, things we can't understand, things we do understand happening to us, happening to others close and far away

Our walk with Jesus will not be easy at all points in our lives but they will have a lesson to learn, we will have consequences to face, we will touch others' lives! Stay the race, for it will never be the worst in history that has ever been.

John 3:16 (NIV)

> ¹⁶For God so loved the world that he gave his one and only son, that whoever believes in him shall not perish but have eternal life. ¹⁷For God did not send his son into the world to condemn the world, but to save the world through him.

What will you do, what will you accomplish that will honor Jesus for what he has done for us, sure we wine, we hurt, we see suffering, but that is, the hand of a child that gets burned on the stove top and Jesus has gently reached down to us and held us close to him and said I am there with you always until the end of time...

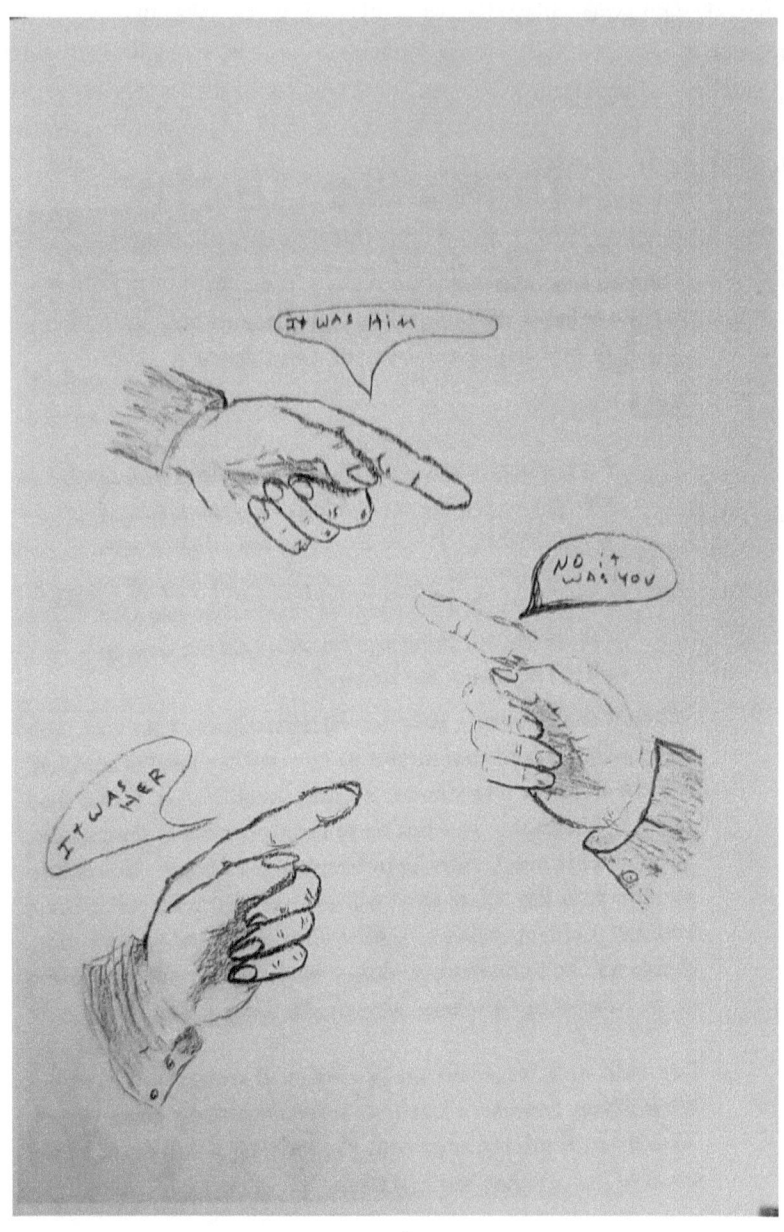

RAW

The Church and Christianity is not what Christ wanted, as some may believe. We are to pick up our cross daily and follow him, that is the church. To follow Him or his ways and to go out to the world and be as he was when he walked in the flesh to us, to be among the people, to *pray*: that means to talk to God, converse with him, just like you would if you were talking to your earthly father. Listen and follow his instruction by teaching his words.

We need to use him as an example after all that is what he was, is, and always will be to this world and to what a lot of people consider "misfits of humanity."

Christianity was not what Jesus invented. What did he say, I will make you Christians? No he said follow me and I will make you fishers of men.

Matthew. 4:19–20 (KJV):

> [19]And he saith unto them, Follow me, and I will make you fishers of men. [20]And they straightway left *their* nets, and followed him.
> (and we will go to church), I don't think so!

Mark 16:14–18: (KJV):(The Great Commission), 16 Then the eleven disciples went away into Galilee, into a mountain where Jesus had appointed them. 17And when they saw him, they worshipped him: but some doubted.

18And Jesus came and spake unto them, saying, All power is given unto me in heaven and in earth. 19Go ye therefore, and teach all nations, baptizing them in the name of the Father, and of the Son, and of the Holy Ghost: 20Teaching them to observe all things whatsoever I have commanded you: and, lo, I am with you always, *even* unto the end of the world. Amen

Don't get me wrong, a building (church) is needed for the right purpose in mind, heart, and body. It should not be exploited as anything other than a sanctuary or meeting of hearts and souls, the saved, the unsaved, for the purpose of fellowship and the invitation into the flock of Jesus Christ. But the real work is "out there"!

Christianity is a word, a label, and in some cases has become the abuse of what Jesus / God wants. Christianity has become the church to many followers of Jesus. It has become a box, it has become nothing but a confined place to many (nothing gets in and nothing gets out).

The place to worship is not just a building; it can be done anywhere, any place, and it is in the hearts, souls, and minds of people everywhere.

Romans 12:4–8: (KJV):

> 4For as we have many members in one body, and all members have not the same office: 5So we, being many, are one body in Christ, and every one members one of another. 6Having then gifts differing according to the grace that is given to us, whether prophecy, let us prophesy according to the proportion of faith; 7Or ministry, let us wait on our ministering: or he that teaches, on teaching; 8Or he that exhorts, on exhortation: he that gives, let him do it with simplicity; he that rules, with diligence; he that shows mercy, with cheerfulness.

Jesus sent us out, not to be put into a building or alone by ourselves, but to allow others to share in the message.

You need to be the message of today by telling his story and relate it to yours. That is the way to bring others to Christ, and that is what the church is according to Jesus, and if you want to label it "that is what Christianity is supposed to be, then and now, thank you, Jesus."

When following Jesus you must leave everything behind and follow him (does that sound familiar). Refer to:

Matt. 10:37–39; Matt. 16:24–28; Mark 8:34–38 and of course

Luke 9:23-25 (KJV):

> [23] And he said to *them* all, If any *man* will come after me, let him deny himself, and take up his cross daily, and follow me. [24] For whosoever will save his life shall lose it: but whosoever will lose his life for my sake, the same shall save it. [25] For what is a man advantaged, if he gain the whole world, and lose himself, or be cast away?

In mind, in body, in spirit, "Walk the Walk," "Talk the Talk," and believe in what he is, and what he wants for us. It is all for the love of Jesus, and what greater gift can men do for the world. I will let scripture say it:

John 15:13-17 (AKJV)

> [13] Greater love has no man than this, that a man lay down his life for his friends. [14] You are my friends, if you do whatever I command you. [15] From now on I call you not servants; for the servant knows not what his Lord does: but I have called you friends; for all things that I have

> heard of my Father I have made known to you. ¹⁶You have not chosen me, but I have chosen you, and ordained you, that you should go and bring forth fruit, and that your fruit should remain: that whatever you shall ask of the Father in my name, he may give it you. ¹⁷These things I command you, that you love one another.

And the heart of Jesus in this of course: John 3:16–17 (KJV):

> ¹⁶For God so loved the world, that he gave his only begotten Son, that whosoever believeth in him should not perish, but have everlasting life. ¹⁷For God sent not his Son into the world to condemn the world; but that the world through him might be saved

Never lose sight of the Lord in anything you do or say!

In closing, God is working through you right now and always has but you probably know that by now. Pray to him for guidance that means *talk to him on a daily basis*. "You need to *act, move, reach out to others,* don't let them slip away." Write down what he has put in your heart, start a journal so you don't lose his thoughts, his perfect words that he is communicating to you personally. He has a plan for everyone if you listen to and for it; after all, if you write down your ideas as I have, they won't slip away.

Do you think your words are more important than His? If he were trying to warn you about an approaching disaster, wouldn't that be more interesting than your own thoughts?

His Words, His gifts to you, His ideas to all through you, don't let them slip away! After all we are the Body of Christ. "Share it just as I have with you: just as God has with me"!

Gods Posts

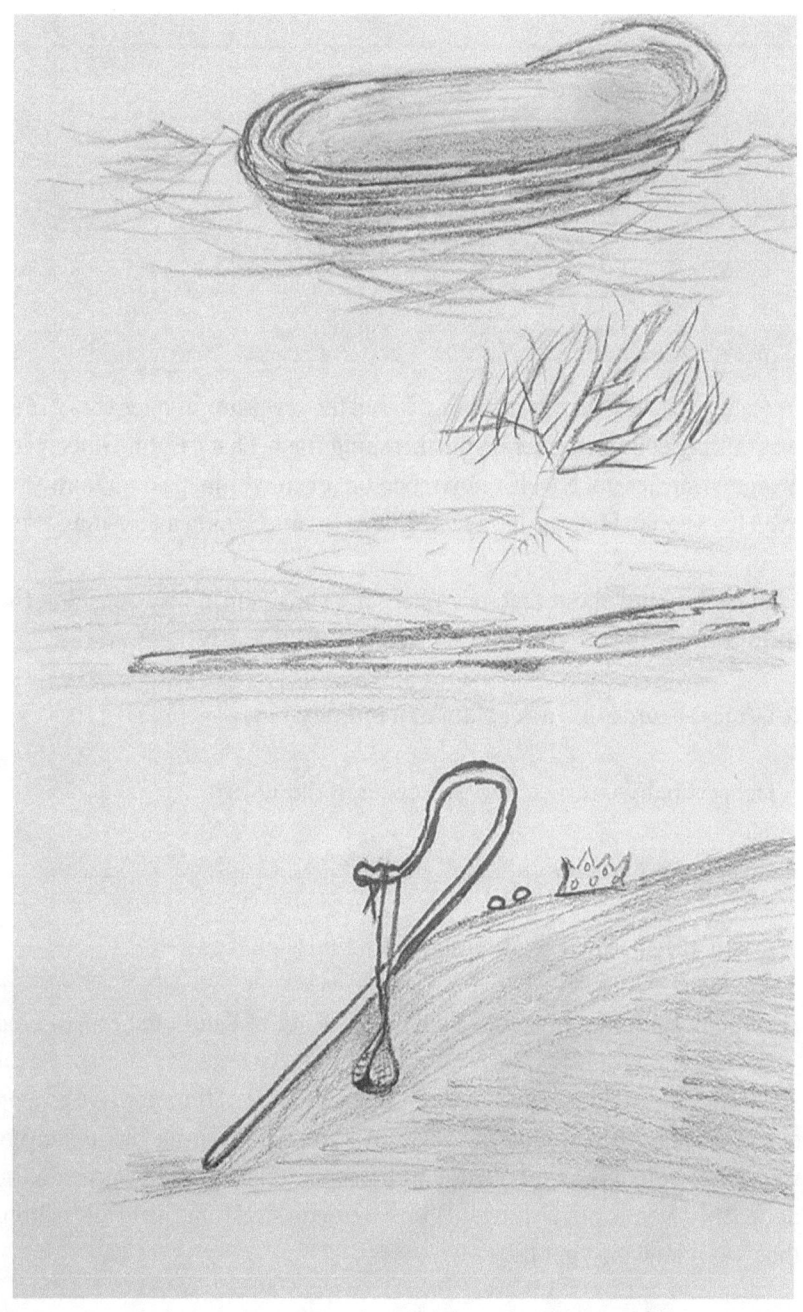

The "Ordinary," "Out of the Ordinary"

In reading the lesson this morning, I read the scripture, Judges 6:11–16; it was talking about a farmer on the threshing floor. That's right, Gideon and ordinary farmer not a well-known person, even within his own family, or even his people. He was just an "ordinary" man cleaning a threshing floor.

I got to thinking about that, or rather "the Holy Spirit," was pushing the thoughts around my mind like he does frequently!

A farmer —turns into a "captain of a military"

A Hebrew baby—turned into a "Leader of the Jews"

A shepherd—turns into a "king"

A group of fishermen—turn into the first missionaries

A carpenter's son—turns into a shepherd, King of Kings, the Son of God

He shows up within us and makes us stand out for Him; not like a neon sign that says, "I Am God the King of Kings!" No sorta, like a simple, wooden "Welcome" sign outside of a Carpenters Hut, with a note on the door, "My Son is out fishing." If or when you find him, just follow him, that way you won't get lost!

I'm ordinary, were all ordinary; what's he got planned for us? It will be an adventure I'm sure.

What army will you lead when he asks? What crowd will gather when you speak, and will you speak when he asks you to? When the Holy Spirit prompts you to, what influence will you make on the masses, or crowd, or that one person that may make all the difference in the world?

If you believe in anything enough to stand your ground, and tell the people about it; isn't time to use that courage that God gave you, to speak out for the one who gave you that courage in the first place?

Romans 8:30-32 (NASB):

> [30]and these whom He predestined, He also called; and these whom He called, He also justified; and these whom He justified, He also glorified. [31]What then shall we say to these things? If God is for us, who is against us? [32]He who did not spare His own Son, but delivered Him over for us all, how will He not also with Him freely give us all things?

"WELCOME"

My Son is out Fishing, If or when you find him, just Follow him, that way you will never get lost!

God CO: JC

Fishin Without a Net

Fishing our way and fishing when you let the Lord cast the line for you are two entirely different things.

Matthew 4:19 19. *"Come, follow Me, Jesus said, "and I will make you fishers of men."*

When I was young I used to fish every chance I got and If I didn't have a pole I would find the means to make something that would get the job done and you'd be surprised at what people would leave behind. If there were old snags where someone broke the line I'd wade out and dislodge them from whatever rock or trash they were hooked on and use that for the line, and then it was just a matter of finding a good tree limb. You could find lures, hooks and sinkers, sometimes you would get real lucky when the water got low and find a slew of things sometimes even a whole pole and reel. Now that's recycling if I've ever seen it.

Mark 6:7-8, [7]**Calling the Twelve to him, he began to send them out two by two and gave them authority over impure spirits.** [8]**These were his instructions: "Take nothing for the journey except a staff--no bread, no bag, no money in your belts.**

I used to love using a bobber in really quiet waters and watch the ripples around it when I would get a bite. The thrill of what might be biting at the bait and the fight of bringing one in. It reminds me of my ship after pulling out of dry-dock. We had to perform checks on all equipment before going back out to sea. One night I was on the "Focsle," that's what they called the front of the ship. It was at night and myself and another sailor were looking over the front and the sides of the ship at all the Jellyfish moving around about two stories down in the water. After about five minutes of looking we saw these ripples forming a perfect circle starting from one side around the front to the other side continuously at about 2 to 3 minute intervals. About the time I figured out what this was all about I noticed that every time the ripples went out all the fish would jump out of the water where the ripples came to an end. As It turned out, it was the ships sonar that was being tested. It was because the water was so calm at night.

This is reminder to me of how everything we do now and will ever do will affect other's that are in our line of sight or in our path. That is what our Lord intended for us. His, is a carefully planned out strategy for our lives to benefit others for His Kingdom.

Another scripture comes to mind when I think about baiting the hook. **Cor. 9:21-23 21.** *[21]To those not having the law I became like one not having the law (though I am not free from God's law but am under Christ's law), so as to win those not having the law. 22. [22]To the weak I became weak, to win the weak. I have become all things to all people so that by all possible means I might save some. [23]I do all this for the sake of the gospel, that I may share in its blessings.*

I loved going out after a rainy day and catching Night crawlers. Ya see, in order to be good at it you had to have a flashlight and just flash them long enough to see where they are, then you reach down and carefully grab them at the hole they came out of and slowly pull them out without breaking them. That sort of reminds me of how Paul preached to all kinds of people. He had been in those situations before, he knew how they thought and he knew their way's because he had been there, so why not use that for God. If we are fishing without God we are fishing without a net, Just like a tightrope walker, there are more chances to make a mistake without being prepared for the outcome.

YFICA

Sunrise-vs-Sonset, Did You Ever Wonder

Sinners to Saints, we are like earth is to water,
or sky is to the world.
I was watching the sun go down and the Holy Spirit
was with me as I started to
understand the grand scheme of things as
God had created and presented them to me.
As the Sun creating a beautiful sunset,
So we should all be reminded that God sent
his only Son here to save us from our sins
by adopting us into the Kingdom of the
most high. Those of us that have been at Sea or
from a beach have become
witnesses to this sunset which I believe is witness to
Jesus Christ's Baptism every night!
Just as we are witness to this, there is the
Holy Birth of Jesus Christ into this
world; The morning brings the remembrance,
and message of His sacrifice and
Crucifixion for us as well.
The sunrise also reminds us of the Son being raised
from the dead and resurrected.
If we believe in Jesus Christ and all he has done,
we will meet Him when He comes to take us home

GIFTS

Everyone in this world has a job, had a job, or will have a job! Whatever that job is, you are actually training for something bigger than you as the worker realize. It is a bigger picture than that.

You may be a carpenter, cook, mechanic, or even in the military. Wherever you are, whatever the job, God has a purpose that He has included into that job that you will make a living with. I know that's a shocker, because you thought the only reason for work was to work for a living! The Lord plans everything on this earth, the how, what, where, when, and why. It will eventually affect everybody in one way or another. When you were, or will become "born again" believer in Jesus Christ, you become a part of the Body of Christ just like a bolt is to an engine, or like your hand is to your arm.

1 Corinthians. 12:12–27:

> [12]Just as a body, though one, has many parts, but all its many parts form one body, so it is with Christ. [13]For we were all baptized by[a] one Spirit so as to form one body—whether Jews or Gentiles, slave or free—and we were all given the one Spirit to drink. [14]Even so the body is not made up of one part but of many.
>
> [15]Now if the foot should say, "Because I am not a hand, I do not belong to the body," it would not for that reason

stop being part of the body. ¹⁶And if the ear should say, "Because I am not an eye, I do not belong to the body," it would not for that reason stop being part of the body. ¹⁷If the whole body were an eye, where would the sense of hearing be? If the whole body were an ear, where would the sense of smell be? ¹⁸But in fact God has placed the parts in the body, every one of them, just as he wanted them to be. ¹⁹If they were all one part, where would the body be? ²⁰As it is, there are many parts, but one body.

²¹The eye cannot say to the hand, "I don't need you!" And the head cannot say to the feet, "I don't need you!" ²²On the contrary, those parts of the body that seem to be weaker are indispensable, ²³and the parts that we think are less honorable we treat with special honor. And the parts that are unpresentable are treated with special modesty, ²⁴while our presentable parts need no special treatment. But God has put the body together, giving greater honor to the parts that lacked it, ²⁵so that there should be no division in the body, but that its parts should have equal concern for each other. ²⁶If one part suffers, every part suffers with it; if one part is honored, every part rejoices with it.

²⁷Now you are the Body of Christ, and each one of you is a part of it.

Jesus set the perfect example by living in the flesh here on earth.

He was born under the worst conditions. He lived a sinless life within the noblest of blood. He was brought to trial and condemned by the ones he came to save, and then He died one of the most excruciating deaths, forgiving those who mocked him even while He hung on the cross in which with His dying breath asked forgiveness for the very ones that had put him there. That forged the way to His resurrection and our forgiveness for all our sins for all time if we only believe and ask forgiveness for them. Then we can be with Him in heaven, when we die an eternity with Him, sinless and new.

Now back to your job and what it really has to do with you!

"So you want to be a cook": The example is that of a cook, when you finally figure out and are comfortable in cooking you are prepared to go out into the world and do that job, right? So say your baking a cake, you must first lay out the ingredients, without the ingredients you can't do much of anything; but when you mix the proper amounts together and cook them, you should have a cake.

That is how it is with the Holy Spirit! He applies His ingredients or influence into you for a purpose.

Let's say it's your daughter, son, granddaughter or grandson. We all love them, we all want to give them hope for the future and teach them to have faith so that they may believe. Well that's the cake and the cake in this example is your kids or grandchildren, our friends, coworkers, any and every one we come into contact with. All these, we want accepted to the family of Christ.

So this may give you a better perspective of another subject when speaking of a job "Money." Before you think about how important that is to your life, and making a living, ask yourself this question which is more important money or your children, or grandchildren.

While the scripture speaks of money as in Luke!

Luke 16:13:

> "No one can serve two masters. Either you will hate the one and love the other, or you will be devoted to the one and despise the other. You cannot serve both God and money."

It also speaks of what's important to rely on such as in Matthew.

Matthew 6:28-30:

> [28]"And why are you worried about clothing? Observe how the lilies of the field grow; they do not toil nor do they spin, [29]Yet I say to you that not even Solomon in all his glory clothed himself like one of these. [30]If that is how God clothes the grass of the field, which is alive today and tomorrow is thrown into the furnace, will he not much more clothe you—you of little faith?
>
> Money is only evil if you misuse it.

Now That's What I'm Talkin' About

There have been a few times that I have gotten a nudge or two to talk to someone I may not even know or go someplace I have didn't plan to go. It's usually a conversation that I am not prepared for and it goes places that I'm not ready for. That's right I am not eloquent in speech, I cannot pick out the perfect words that get attention but I know that God does.

That is why I get so excited after one of these experiences has played out for someone and for me. The pure genius of our Lord to give us an interpreter as he did with the Holy Spirit. I also get a prompting to write these things down. I can't seem to stop until I am finished and sometimes it is so overwhelming that he cares so much and loves me as to prove his power and purpose to me in these ways.

My heart was hardened because of sin but to me this proves that his grace is sufficient and he will never let me go. So far this is the journey he has led me to. To reach out in his name and help other to come to Christ, to reach out to those that have lost their way, those that think they're lost because of the sin that has burdened them when in fact they are not. Even after some are saved, born again into him they feel lost. This is the proof that all need to hear that we all have sinned and fall short of the glory of God. Thank you Jesus for the sacrifice you have given for us and thank you for the gift of your Holy Spirit.

Gods Posts

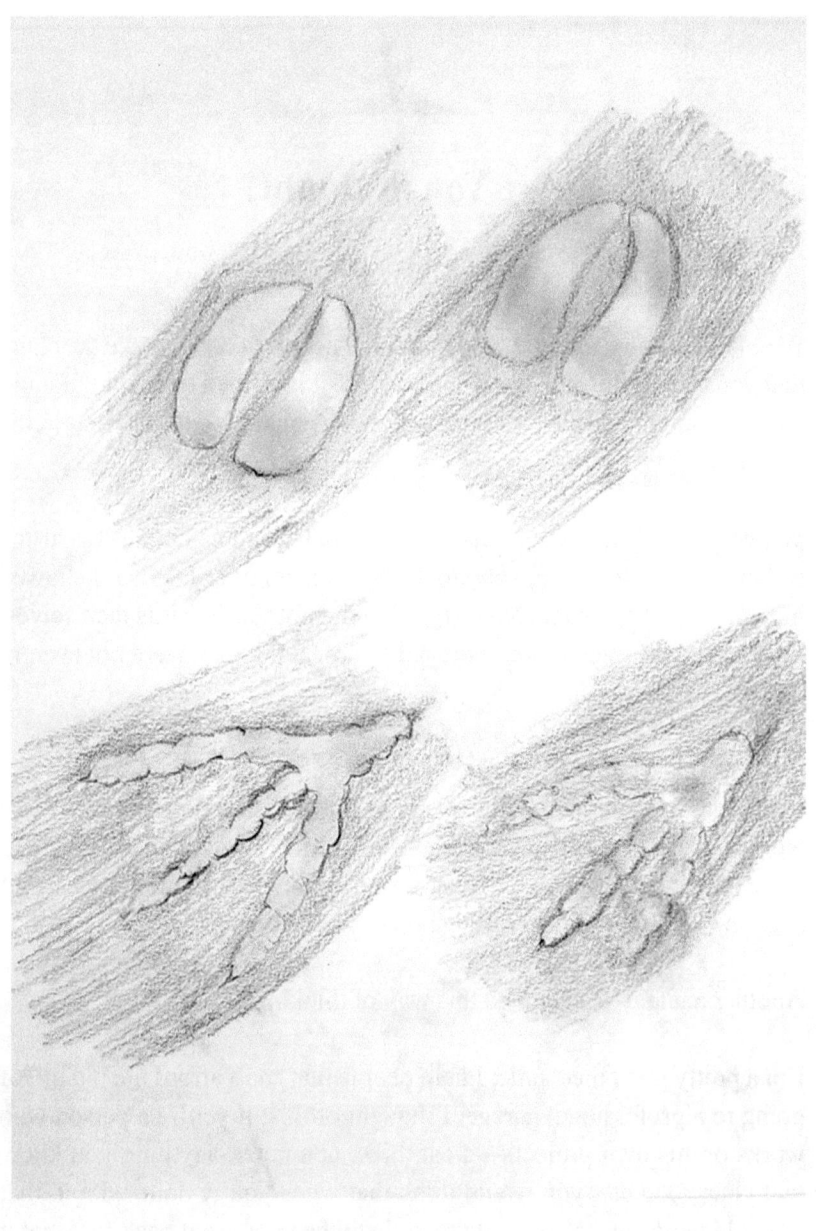

Are You in Doubt?

When I read about atheism, and that some people actually make the claim that you can't believe in the Bible because it is written by man, I thought back to something that was said when I was hunting with a friend in the Mountains of Arizona:

When I was hunting with a friend of mine, he said he couldn't hear the turkey in the woods that were gobbling back at my call. When I showed him the tracks, and some other signs but did not see the birds themselves, he disputed me even more to the point that he felt they were not even In that part of the woods.

So I asked him: "Are there any elk, white tail, or mule deer up here?" He immediately came back with "Of course there is, they're all over these woods!" I said, "How do you know that?" After saying this he just stood there and stared at me, and I just stared back. "I'm assuming the point sunk in," because he never said another word about it.

Another analogy leads me to this way of thinking as well:

I'm a pretty good mechanic; I help people that can't afford the big bill of going to a professional garage. I thought of this; if you're a person who works on his own projects—a car, bike, computer, anything you know that your good at—you would think that when you're done with it, that it would work fine. You would trust that when you went back to it that it would work the way it was supposed to, right?

So if it was a car that you worked on and you know at the end of the day it was done right, it would probably work when you were finished with it that night. You would "believe" that when you put the key in the ignition and turn, it would start!

The question I have for you is this: if you have faith in what you do, and "believe" that your car will start when you use that key, why wouldn't you believe there is a God?

If you are ever in doubt, if you think God doesn't exist, or you feel you just don't hear from God and you really want to hear Him speak to you, all you need to do is open up your heart and mind to him and ask him to speak to you. Read the Bible, and yes, it is true, "men did write the Bible," but it was because the words are God breathed, the words are timeless. When you read them they will take you to where you are in your life. Even though they were written over two thousand years ago, they were always meant for the person who reads them; no matter who you are, or when you need Him, they will be where you need to be. For the Bible truly is "The Living Word"; a constant communicator between us and God. The Holy Spirit will interpret for you if and when you choose to believe. The Holy Spirit dwells in the pages until we ask God to reveal himself to us.

Ya Ever Get the Feeling You're Bein' "Watched"!

We have been going through this misfit crisis lately. Things in our past keep coming back up punchin' holes in our gut. Sometimes it's confusing, sometimes it's wondering what to do next with it. Sometimes we are listening to the wrong voice, again, "that's right, again." Dear Lord, we are not Daniel, we don't see things in our dreams that explain things so vividly. The writings on the wall need to have a signature at the end of the message or at least an initial like contracts or letters have. Like, "Sincerely Yours" J. C. or H. S., or just *God*. Is this really you or am I getting this from the mail room, "you know the lower level." I now understand in a way what Gideon must have been thinking when he tested the Lord's patience. Isn't it easy to sit back and read about the prophet's or the Israeli's constantly asking and winning through their lives about, "Is this really you?" Could you just do this one little thing and I will know it's you. Then you get on this kick "Are you still there?" Every time we do that we need to go to the scriptures and read all the examples that are there. Suddenly the scripture Proverbs 3:3 makes a lot of sense:

Let not mercy and truth forsake thee: bind them about thy neck; write them upon the table of thine heart:

Well the other day my friend and I met in the weirdest of places. I thought he just showed up to help me in an hour of need so to speak, and he did, but after the initial earthly help, there was a deeper help that couldn't have been anyone but our old friend the Holy Spirit, that's right, the trials and tribulations thing again. We spilled out our hearts again about how things were going with us, how we were hurting not knowing what direction to take, what we learned from the Holy Spirit before, and what Jesus meant to us; but most importantly what was tugging at us today, this week, lately. What was bothering us now, what are we whining about, where is God in all this, yea sounds familiar "right," it's the same thing. It's coming from us though it's different, we don't see it because we're not looking at it.

We all keep looking for a sign! Where is God in all this? Is Jesus walking with us or is he just sitting there with Dad watching the show from the bleacher seats? Will we even know when he does answer us? The better question is, are we even listening, or are we to busy asking? Have we thanked him for what he has done? Or are we waiting for the next problem to ask him about in another vicious cycle of me, me, me.

Well I'm here to tell you the good news! Yes, he answers every question we have and I have the proof. You will only understand it if you ask the Lord to help you understand it. Sometimes it's obvious, other times it's a puzzle and there's a reason for that as well, it all has to do with the pieces and those pieces are the lives that are involved and how God is reaching out to them through this puzzle and only then will the puzzle come together.

Please and thank you were taught to you as a kid, the fact that you asked says that you believe there will be a reward, then you say thank you. It works that way with everything especially in your prayers. If you're not grateful for something, how would you feel if this were in the reverse?

The answer to our question or our whining, we or at least I got a message the next day. It came in the form of the devotions as it has before. It had to do with paying too much attention to the turmoil going on inside of each of us and what we do with it. The scripture had to do with one of my favorites Elijah. He went to escape Jezebel after she threatened his life. He didn't commit suicide though, he was right with the Lord, but he was tired of fighting for the end result, especially when it came to a threat like this one, so he wanted the Lord to take him. This was Elijah having a pity party his conscience or the devil was telling him you've done enough; don't subject yourself to facing that monster of a queen. That evil one will give you a slow death and make you suffer. (Sounds terrible to me as well, the way she threatened him wasn't pretty at all.)

Elijah Flees Jezebel—1 Kings 19:1-2 (NASB):

> [1]Now Ahab told Jezebel all that Elijah had done, and how he had killed all the prophets with the sword. [2]Then Jezebel sent a messenger to Elijah, saying, "So may the gods do to me and even more, if I do not make your life as the life of one of them by tomorrow about this time."

So here's the answer; what now I don't understand is what do I do with this. Is that all there is? Oooohh no.

Isaiah 55:11 (KJV) says:

> So shall my word be that goeth forth out of my mouth: it shall not return unto me void, but it shall accomplish that which I please, and it shall prosper in the thing whereto I sent it.

People I don't know where you are in your struggle, but I'm pretty sure you're not traipsing around the desert for forty years (read about Moses in Exodus), or asking the Lord to prove to you that he is there by making the ground wet or dry under a rug, (read about Gideon in Judges), or Daniel who the Lord spoke to or Elijah! But I know the Lord is answering our prayers, our questions. All we need to do is ask and then listen for him to answer, sometimes it isn't right away and sometimes it's not words, watch for it, for whatever form it comes in, be ready and always thank him.

Judges 6:36–40: (always testing His patients)

> ³⁶Then Gideon said to God, "If You will deliver Israel through me, as You have spoken, ³⁷behold, I will put a fleece of wool on the threshing floor. If there is dew on the fleece only, and it is dry on all the ground, then I will know that You will deliver Israel through me, as You have spoken." ³⁸And it was so. When he arose early the next morning and squeezed the fleece, he drained the dew from the fleece, a bowl full of water. ³⁹Then Gideon said to God, "Do not let Your anger burn against me that I may speak once more; please let me make a test once more with the fleece, let it now be dry only on the fleece, and let there be dew on all the ground." ⁴⁰God did so that night; for it was dry only on the fleece, and dew was on all the ground.

Have you ever been around someone who continues your sentence? Sometimes that's the way I feel the Lord is answering me. I start sharing, feeling bad about something I did or said, and pray hard that he will forgive me for my sin. I tear up, I wine about how I feel, and then the Lord puts the example right in front of me, He speaks to me and says there's more to it than just you! I planned the outcome this way, I was just waiting for you to understand it.

What Is This World Coming Too

How many things, subjects, or sins will we give into that will create normality for the human race before we are reduced to nothing but a pagan ritual? There will eventually be no god, no laws, and no rules. Some say we are evolving, and God sees us repeating the past and degrading.

If it hadn't been for Jesus Christ, I would seriously wonder how God could love mankind (to whom he made in his own image). With crimes running ramped, undefined, and unaccounted for, where is the line that was crossed? It is like chalk that has been washed away and it has almost disappeared in a blur.

From everything that we have been taught, disgrace is being turned into popularity! Like music to our ears, we have invited the vilest of words into our vocabulary through our subconscious and we don't even see it coming. The sound is sweet but the words are quietly eating away at how we speak.

Television used to be the way to see around the world, nature, shows about past and present, the laughter of simple comedy, and simple family shows with the basis of right and wrong. Today it has worked its way to a variety of behind the scenes shows without any conscience whatsoever; no dignity, stories of drama without a storyline, or vice versa; all for the sake of catching the eye. Through the ages TV has unlocked the door to untouched words of hatred, violence, bullying, and all types of obscenities. It now teaches our children and grownups how to hate and take revenge, and shows us all how it's done in the name of entertainment. Commercials are showing us which pill or drug will take care of anything from mental health to desires and needs.

If that wasn't enough the computer was invented and with one stroke of a key, oops, you just saw something you know you're not supposed to be looking at! Another investigation into "how did this get there" and you could be hooked. An addition to this are phones we hold in our hands and carry them around in our pockets. They have the same damaging effects as the PC, actually more. Not only can you be mobile with the destruction of your mind, and soul, not to mention your family; these things can cause accidents, even death by texting. The devil has made things soooo easy to fall into!

Questions to ponder:

- If God didn't give us a pass in the garden with Adam and Eve into humanity, where would we be? Or would we be?
- If Abraham was never visited by the holy visitors to be given that miracle of a son between himself and Sara, what would become of our gene pool? What about Muslims?
- If God decided "enough is enough," what more proof do they need? Would there be anyone left of the chosen people? What would Jesus's lineage be in this situation?
- Would there be a Ten Commandments? If Moses didn't listen or if he just said "I understand God, these people don't deserve anything. They're just not satisfied with anything you do for them."

The truth of the matter is this: all the history we know now or are still making cannot happen any other way. Everything we have ever done or will do has already happened in the eyes of the Lord. We can't change it because it has already been written. If we did this, would this happen? If we did that would this happen?

There is a reason why a second of Gods time is as the same as decades of ours!

So how many chances is He going to give us? History shows Him with us time and time again. His love is endless; it is why he created us in the first place. So when are we going to say "enough is enough"? It is time to give it all to Him.

No one is without sin! There has never been anyone, anytime, anywhere that has not sinned in some way, shape or form within the eyes of God except for His Son Jesus Christ.

> *Psalms 139:7–9 NIV says:*
> *Where can I go from your Spirit?*
> *Where can I flee from your presence?*
> *[8]If I go up to the heavens, you are there;*
> *if I make my bed in the depths, you are there.*
> *[9]If I rise on the wings of the dawn,*
> *if I settle on the far side of the sea,*
> *[10]even there your hand will guide me,*
> *your right hand will hold me fast.*

So now there it is, this is our starting point! This isn't a diet, it's not a promise you keep to a friend, it's not a New Year's resolution. It's all about what God wants to do in and with your life. Don't let that fight inside you go on! Ask Jesus into your heart, ask his forgiveness, and believe He will take it all away and make you new today, or again. Do not fight back the convictions. Jesus just wants to love and hold on to you. Ephesians 6:18 praying at all times in the spirit, with all prayer and supplication. To that end keep alert with all perseverance, making supplication for all the saints.

Gods Posts

He gave us the great commission; it wasn't just for the disciples! He intended us all to go out and bring in the harvest throughout the world after giving us His words, with all the answers and all the examples. He wanted us all to be "Fishers of Men"

What God is that Perfect Word

Lord as the mist rolls out of the grass and drifts away.
I ask you Father to show me this new day.
With pen in hand and eyes on you.
I pray lord gift me with words lived through.

For in no way do I live a perfect life.
These hours of beauty are with me in strife.
Grant me father words to other sinners, your truth.
Show them your way, your words that sooth.

For what dear God is your perfect word that be.
That will bring all souls into loves eternity.
For why is your love , that we search for, to find, so hard.
 When so closely to our soul's you guard.

Free will you gave but our love is all you ever asked.
For this you sent your Son who like the fisherman's line you cast.
The living Story that is in your book be told.
Of your son Jesus whose truth given, is so bold.

Gave us those words, healing and much more.
After years of offering up sacrifice from before.
Our Jesus had the answer all along.
To suffer and die on a cross for all our wrong.

All proof that Gods Love conquers all.
In three days, his body had left the tomb as was his call.
For we now have proof of His promise and it is here.
We only need to believe in Jesus, ask forgiveness and then there is no fear.
We know now God is three in one.
He is the father and then the spirit and Jesus the son.

YFICA

www.ingramcontent.com/pod-product-compliance
Lightning Source LLC
LaVergne TN
LVHW091604060526
838200LV00036B/994